Does Truth Matter?

On the Fragility of Truth in an Age of Convenient Lies

Dr. Jean Maalouf

EXCELLER BOOKS®
A GLOBAL PRESS

Does Truth Matter?
On the Fragility of Truth in an Age of Convenient Lies

Cover by Exceller Books using resources from Pixabay.com

Print ISBN: 978-93-48892-70-6

First published in India in 2025 by Exceller Books,
An imprint of GE Group

Address: G1, Dream Apartment, Degree College Road, Belgharia,
Kolkata, 700056, India
www.excellerbooks.com

EXCELLER BOOKS®
A GLOBAL PRESS

Does Truth Matter?

Dedication

To those who rightly replace Pilate's convenient and evasive question, "What is truth?" by the accurate and piercing question "Who is truth?"

And to those who think, say, and live the Truth boldly, fearlessly, and without compromise and complicity.

Reviews

"I've always thought that the most powerful weapon in the world was the bomb and that's why I gave it to my people, but I've come to the conclusion that the most powerful weapon in the world is not the bomb but it's the truth."
—Andrei Sakharov

"Every violation of truth is not only a sort of suicide in the liar, but is a stab at the health of human society."
—Ralph Waldo Emerson

"Who lies for you will lie against you."
—John Locke

"Tell a lie loud enough and long enough and people will believe it."
—Adolf Hitler

"One mark of a deteriorating society is when people cannot discern between truth and lies. Another is that they don't care and will believe whatever their itching ears want to hear."
—Cal Thomas

"I'm not upset that you lied to me, I'm upset that from now on I can't believe you."
—Friedrich Nietzsche

"If you want to be wrong then follow the masses."
—Socrates

"False words are not only evil in themselves, but they infect the soul with evil."
—Plato

"Liars are the cause of all the sins and crimes in the world."

—Epictetus

"No man has a good enough memory to be a successful liar."
—Abraham Lincoln

"A liar is not believed even though he tells the truth."
—Marcus Tullius Cicero

"There are two ways to be fooled. One is to believe what isn't true; the other is to refuse to believe what is true."
—Soren Kierkegaard

"An error does not become truth by reason of multiplied propagation, nor does truth become error because nobody sees it."
—Mahatma Gandhi

"Devotion to Truth is the sole justification for our existence."
—Mahatma Gandhi

"Truth does not change because it is, or is not, believed by a majority of the people."
—Giordano Bruno

"Lying lips are an abomination to the Lord, but those who act faithfully are his delight."
—Proverbs 12:22

"You can beat 40 scholars with one fact, but you cannot beat one idiot with 40 facts."
— Jalal ad-Din Muhammad Rumi

"Let your word be 'Yes, Yes' or 'No, No' anything more than this comes from the evil one."
—Matthew 5:37

"Jesus said to him, "I am the way, and the truth, and the life."
—John 14:6

Contents

Introduction

Truth is one of the first casualties of our modern life. The question "Is it true?" has become, sadly, "Whose truth is it?" People tend to live by their beliefs—even if their beliefs are not true.

Practically, truth seems to have lost its correlation with reality, becoming mere plausibility or, especially, an effort to obtain a certain desired effect. It is mainly used to confirm an agenda or carry out a mission. We no longer discover truth; we create the truth that is in our image. We easily twist our perceptions and make our opponents look bad in order to promote ourselves and meet our needs and interests. It is even worse when, while refusing to acknowledge any valid truth in the other side's position, we monopolize the right to truth as if "the doctrine of infallibility" has moved to our side—as if we were immune to flaws, inconsistencies, and shortsightedness.

No wonder we've made our world one of spin, bias, and well-established excessive relativism.

Yet, in the heart of our hearts, we know that without truth, nothing is worth living or dying for. This is why the pursuit of truth has been, still is, and will always be a widely shared project of humankind. There is, and will always be, an urgent need for people of truth. We know there is no other way to live free and be fully human.

But if, in the depths of our hearts, we greatly love and appreciate truth, why then do we lie almost spontaneously? Why does the epidemic of cheating cover all segments of society? Why are we so apathetic in the face of hypocrisy? More importantly, how can we free ourselves from lies to become men and women of truth?

This book will try to answer these questions and many more, and help us become aware of the danger of lying and deceiving, which affects faith, marriages, children, relationships, careers, and every aspect of our lives. Above all, it will show the biblical path toward greater truthfulness, integrity, and honesty—dearly treasured, but such rare virtues.

Also, this book will ask questions—even uncomfortable ones—that force our hidden motivations to come out into the open and reveal our need to ask God's help to heal unhealed wounds and be free from false selves and untruths.

Strangely and paradoxically, we seem to live in a tell-all culture. We are free to confess our feelings, our frustrations, our shyness, our failures, our indiscretions, and our struggles to wake up and go on with our lives.

Yet, politicians lie to get elected, doctors lie on reports, scientists fabricate data, professionals and experts distort facts and events, CEOs of corporations cook the books, journalists twist news, universities lie about athletes, advertisers lie about products, ordinary citizens lie on income tax returns, and pastors lie about money and private lives. In all these cases, truth is so stretched that reality is recognizable no more, and cheating becomes the common currency—justified by an "everybody's-doing-it" rationale. Consequently, there is no surprise in seeing ourselves immersed in various forms of equivocation, cover-up, camouflage, delusion, complicity of inaction, and—even worse—we try to mitigate any attempt at accountability from and to anyone.

Don't you think we are clearly out of alignment with what is good, true, right, and real?

Finding the foundation by which all truths must be judged is essential. Jesus pointed to this unshakable rock. He said, "I am the way, and the truth, and the life" (John 14:6)—that is, according to the author of the Letter to the Hebrews, "The same yesterday and today and forever" (Hebrews 13:8).

Truth is definitely the decisive issue of our time, because without it, freedom is merely an illusory mirage and a self-serving fantasy. Only when we accept Jesus' invitation to "Put out into the deep water" (Luke 5:4) will we discover more of God's truth—and realize how "The truth will make [us] free" (John 8:32), as Jesus said.

Everyone is in search of truth. And to think that only philosophers, scientists, and religious exponents and advocates are entitled to seek the truth would be wrong. Deep in their very hearts, people are eager for certainty, even in the midst of uncertainties, chaotic environments, and contradictory propositions. However, due to the imperfection of human nature, it does not seem easy for humans to draw a clear line between certainties and possibilities, between clarity and doubt, between truth and untruth, and between plausibility and post-truth.

Does truth matter? Of course it does. Even though many people think lies, say lies, and live lies, truth should be well conceived, boldly told, and fearlessly lived—and be it, no matter what and no matter the cost. This book will tell you how.

Part 1: The Post Truth World Order

"You can beat 40 scholars with one fact, but you cannot beat one idiot with 40 facts."

— *Jalal ad-Din Muhammad* Rumi

1 | Toward a Post-Truth World Order

Everyone, as reality shows, has one thing or another to sell. Everyone tries to persuade others to accept his or her ideas because he or she claims to know what is true and what is not.

How do we really know truth? Is our knowledge of truth a product of the mind—a priori, or before experience—or is it rather the fruit of factual inquiry—a posteriori, or after experience?

Why do people see the same thing in different ways?

The Crisis of Truth: Rationalist and Empiricist Traditions

Rationalist and empiricist schools have been debating this for centuries. The rationalist belief seeks to prove that there are certain fundamental principles or axioms that can be known through reason and that other truth can be deduced from those principles. The empiricist approach argues that one cannot arrive at factual truth by reasoning alone, but by experimenting. Truth about this world, they say, should be an a posteriori event.

How can we consider as a principle, for example, the statement that "All human beings are born free and equal," as a rationalist would like to believe, if so many people are still neither free nor equal, as an empiricist would like to ask?

There is no clear-cut answer to such questions. This is why we find great names of thinkers taking sides in both traditions. In the rationalist tradition, we see names such as

Plato, St. Augustine, René Descartes, Benedict Spinoza, Gottfried Wilhelm Leibniz, and Georg Wilhelm Friedrich Hegel. In the empiricist tradition, we see names such as Aristotle, St. Thomas Aquinas, Sir Francis Bacon, Thomas Hobbes, John Locke, George Berkeley, David Hume, and John Stuart Mill. Blaise Pascal then observed in a famous phrase: "Truth on one side of the Pyrenees; error on the other."

Does this mean that nothing is absolutely this or absolutely that—that everything always has at least two sides, and that no firm distinctions can be easily drawn in life? Indeed, this is what the early Greek philosophers thought. Heraclitus and the Sophists stand behind Protagoras' famous phrase, "Man is the measure of all things." This means that truth is relative to each individual. It also means that a person could defend any position as well as any other, since nothing is absolute. So, what one knows as truth is what one perceives, and what one perceives does not depend on anyone else's perception.

Such a position, which has the appearance of being true, did not convince Socrates and all the "Socrates" after him throughout the centuries until this very day. A Socrates would say that Protagoras' position is self-contradictory and self-defeating, because if truth comes from one's perception only, how can one claim that his or her perception is better than anyone else's? Therefore, what could one teach anyone else at all? Socrates said: "If truth is only sensation… why, my friend, should Protagoras be preferred to the place of wisdom and instruction, and deserve to be well paid, and we poor ignoramuses have to go to him, if each one is the measure of his own wisdom?" Furthermore, if a person thinks that

Protagoras is wrong, then this person must be right—precisely because of the view of Protagoras himself.

This discussion took place about 2,400 years ago and has gone on and on throughout the centuries until today. The essence of any conversation is: "What is truth?" Is it what agrees with the facts? Is it what is consistent with an established corpus of knowledge, a system of judgments, and a set of values? Is it what works, succeeds, and produces positive results and happy endings? Is oneself, or some other authority, the essential ingredient of it?

To these questions, we have modern answers that belong to many schools of thought. The names of some of these schools are very familiar to us, and they belong to every culture and religion. They are: fundamentalism, fanaticism, individualism, traditionalism, exclusivism, absolutism, legalism, literalism, collectivism, far-right-ism, universalism, relativism, and pluralism. They also are: liberalism, laxism, inclusivism, contextualism, situational ethics, far-left-ism, radicalism, modernism, postmodernism, pick-and-choose-ism, black-and-white-ism, either/or-ism, both/and-ism, everybody's-doing-it-ism, and possibly many more under even more sophisticated names.

So, how do we know the truth if partiality and the bias of individual perception are inherent to the human condition? How do we know the truth if time, space, and circumstances impose filters on our perspectives? How do we know the truth when many of us refer to the principle of 'complementarity', which says, "A great truth is a statement whose opposite is also a great truth"? How do we know the truth if no knowledge is final and one of our main problems is the arrogance of ignorance?

Felipe Fernández-Armesto, member of the Modern History Faculty of Oxford University, wrote in his book *Truth: A History and a Guide for the Perplexed*:

> In the twentieth-century West, truth was buried in what I call 'the graveyard of certainty'—a civilization of crumbling confidence, in which it was hard to be sure of anything. Uncertainty was part of a vast scientific counter-revolution, which overthrew the ordered image of the universe inherited from the past and substituted the image we live with today: chaotic, contradictory, full of unobservable events, untrackable particles, untraceable causes and unpredictable effects.

But even if time, space, and circumstances impose filters and perspectives on the way we know the truth; even if we live in a world of our own creation and believe our own lies; and even if our mental capacities vary greatly from culture to culture—does this mean that uncertainties and chaos are the final answer to "What is truth?" Not necessarily. Philosopher Martin Heidegger (1889–1976) suggests that if we cannot *be* the truth, we cannot *know* the truth. To know the truth, one must live it and be it.

However, leaving all this behind, we seem to have reached, at the present time, a point where a "post-truth" approach appears to have taken the prominent position of dictating how we should think, speak, and live.

Philosophy of Post-Truth

The Oxford Dictionaries selected "post-truth" as the word of the year 2016 and defined it as "a term relating to or denoting circumstances in which objective facts are less influential in shaping public opinion than appeals to emotion and personal belief." Such a description seems about right for where we are at the present time. Feelings, fantasies, personal opinions, biases, self-interests, extreme relativism—that's what dictates our behaviors. Not arguments. Not facts. People, then, are allowed to believe whatever they want to believe as long as they feel, believe, and think it is right. As a result, no one believes anything anymore, for the objective truth is replaced by the hundreds of opinions and interpretations conveyed to individual minds through personal mass media. Thus, everything becomes speculation, and nothing is fact—a fact will depend on how one sees it and feels about it, and not on what is. Opinion—how one feels about things—is worth more than the facts. Personal stories are made all the time. Everything is relative, and there is no such thing as the truth. Here comes to mind Blaise Pascal's line, "People almost invariably arrive at their beliefs not on the basis of proof but on the basis of what they find attractive." For post-truth adherents, facts are irrelevant and by far less important than individual beliefs, opinions, and personal agendas. What is also remarkable is that adherents to post-truth are usually immune to being corrected, no matter how obvious the evidence is. Correction is not only rejected, but it might enrage them to the point of using violence against the accusers.

Although the concept of "post-truth" is not new, this concept has emerged and gained prominence in a particular way at the present time. It is remarkable how leaders, especially politicians, lie and make their lies sound truthful. And what is more remarkable is the fact that these leaders are the first to know well that they are lying and are in a hurry to convince the public that they are doing all they can to serve the public. Such leaders, like a good majority of us, have the ability to create stories, then believe them and make the public believe them as well. As human beings, being storytelling individuals must have been an essential part of our journey throughout the centuries. Weren't we?

What makes things worse in this regard is the fact that our present age of technology does not allow us to settle down and think thoroughly. We are continuously driven by market forces that lead us sometimes far from rationality and common sense. We then live our lives according to how we were told to live and according to circumstances. And who cares about truth! Post-truth does not care about truth. What is true is what we believe, say, and do, regardless of the way things and facts actually are. Whether we are aware of it or not, the truth is that we believe, say, and do what high tech has manufactured for us. No one doubts that after we've created Google, Apple, Facebook, Amazon, Twitter, Instagram, YouTube, and many others, we are no longer the same, and our truth is no longer the same. The truth they manufactured has become a reality. And this is the new reality. By the way, when we use the word "post-truth," the prefix "post" does not necessarily refer to what happens "after" truth. It could rather mean that the truth has become obsolete, no longer essential, and has been replaced with a new reality. Here, it would be useful to make a distinction between a liar and a post-truther. By telling a lie, the liar knows there is a truth, knows what the truth is, and goes on telling a different story. The post-truther questions, or even denies, the very fact in a way that undermines the possibility of talking about truth. Truth is simply replaced with another reality altogether. In this context, scientific truth can be easily delegitimized, religious doctrine invalidated, ethical rules rejected, institutional law nullified, and historic events disregarded. In the post-truth era, humanity is facing the lost truth reality in which the lie becomes normal, common, and expected.

2 | On Our Biases

Most of us, if not all of us, think and act in biased ways, but no one wants to admit to being biased. It is always the other who is biased. We usually do this unconsciously and, sometimes, consciously and on purpose.

Biases, partly unconscious and partly conscious, tend to greatly affect the inequality that exists in our society. Think, for example, about how we deal with gender, race, nationality, job, position, privilege, possession, appearance, and the like. Think about the news channels we watch, the books we read, the magazines we subscribe to, the music we listen to, and the movies we watch. Think about our favorite stores, restaurants, and the vehicles we drive. Think about our selected circles of friends.

At what point can we determine the innocence of our choices, and at what point can we say that they are the result of our biases? What is bias? One of the definitions of bias is proposed by Wikipedia, the free encyclopedia. It says:

> **Bias** is a disproportionate weight in favor of or against an idea or thing, usually in a way that is inaccurate, closed-minded, prejudicial, or unfair. Biases can be innate or learned.
>
> People may develop biases for or against an individual, a group, or a belief. In science and engineering, a bias is a systematic error. Statistical

> bias results from an unfair sampling of a population, or from an estimation process that does not give accurate results on average.

With such a definition, one can feel the weight of the bias components—affective ones, cognitive ones, and behavioral ones. That explains all kinds of prejudice, feelings (negative and positive), stereotypes, generalizations, and discrimination toward persons, groups, ideas, opinions, attitudes, and the like.

No matter how we go around and stretch our imaginations to find the right reasons to justify a bias, the obvious truth seems to remain the same: it is the self-serving bias. Even "photograph" facts can be perceived in a way that allows us to see ourselves and our actions not only in the most positive and advantageous light one can imagine, but also as the very center of discernment and judgment on how things are supposed to be judged. In such a case, truth becomes what, consciously or unconsciously, we believe it is. No other reference is allowed to dictate what it should be.

When people are asked if what they said is true, they usually answer with a resounding yes. But when they are asked how they know it's true, they find themselves in the exploratory territory of the objective facts, the possible beliefs, the environmental conditions of religions and cultures, and the subjective feelings and perceptions that can lead to illusory assumptions. No wonder, then, if we become driven by biases toward people, things, organizations, parties, groups, behaviors, and anything that affects our own lives and the lives of others.

Without necessarily knowing it, our mind filters out the information that does not vibrate with our preexisting beliefs and ideas. We seem very often to already have a certain opinion about another race, another religion, another nation, another party, before we make an effort to research who and what they really are. An unconscious phenomenon in us would put the other in a certain category before having a chance to be in contact with that other. Are we the measure of all things? Who gave us the right to be that way? Where does that illusory superiority come from? Why do we see what we want to see? Are we sure of our "truth"?

3 | On Our Fantasist Truths

Truth first or facts first? The answer to this question makes all the difference in the philosophy of existence. Truth is not physically measurable; kindness cannot be weighed on a scale. Facts must be perceived in order to attain truth. But what would happen if we only count on the perception of facts? When we reduce principles to mere feelings and visible facts, much is lost.

Relativism

The sentence "Truth is relative," which we hear everywhere we turn, is itself relative, in spite of its originally intended reality that was meant to be absolute and objective. If one says, "What's true for you may not be true for other people," with the intention of convincing others that this is an absolute truth, one is contradicting himself or herself—since there is no absolute truth, as he or she just claimed. Isn't it contradictory to say there are absolutely no absolutes? So what? Contradictory or not, irrational or not, who cares—provided one satisfies one's own ego and desires.

At the present time, we seem to need a personal possessive pronoun in our ordinary language. We replaced "the truth" with "my truth," "your truth," "their truths." There is no objective truth; there is only subjective truth because reality is a "mental construct," and all truth is dependent on one's perspective.

In any case, we have to admit that relativism is so deeply ingrained in the mindsets and lifestyles of modern men and women that one frequently hears in regular conversations, "Each person should decide for himself or herself what is right and what is wrong, and what is good and what is evil."

So, how to define relativism? The *Cambridge Dictionary* says it is "the belief that truth and right and wrong can only be judged in relation to other things and that nothing can be true or right in all situations." The *Stanford Encyclopedia of Philosophy* says: "Relativism, roughly put, is the view that truth and falsity, right and wrong, standards of reasoning, and procedures of justification are products of differing conventions and frameworks of assessment and that their authority is confined to the context giving rise to them." The *Britannica Dictionary* says that relativism is "the belief that different things are true, right, etc., for different people or at different times." *The Free Dictionary* says that relativism is "the theory that value judgments, as of truth, beauty, or morality, have no universal validity but are valid only for the persons or groups holding them."

Practically, these definitions lead to the following conclusion: what is true or false for you is true or false for you, and not for me, and we should restrain ourselves from telling others that they are wrong because there is no right and wrong. Truth requires a "North Star" for guidance and criteria for verification and falsification. If there is no "North Star" and no criteria, one enters the confusing post-truth approach.

Relativism can infiltrate our total being; it is pervasive in our culture today. We can have, for example, ethical/moral relativism, which wants to submit all morals to the social group within which they are practiced. We can also have cognitive relativism, which believes that there is no system of truth that is more valid and legitimate than another one, that there is no objective standard of truth, and consequently, that there is no God of absolute truth. Also, we can have what is called situational relativism, which means that right and wrong are dependent upon the situation and the circumstances in which we find ourselves.

Relativism can extend to any area of life. This includes all religious convictions and traditions, all art forms, all political systems, all life decisions and lifestyles, etc. This means that principles are based on culture and individual choice, for there are no objective rules governing right and wrong. Therefore, since there is no such thing as objective, historic, real truth, individuals and groups can spin any story according to their own interests, and no one is allowed to judge others—who am I to judge you, and who are you to judge me? And in case of severe disagreements and conflicts, just find a court willing to support your "right."

Moreover, in the sphere of religion—and because all religions are said to be good—if a religion makes a genuine truth-claim at the expense of another religion, that religion is called "intolerant."

Although relativism may be one of the most destructive currents of our times, there is another side to it that should be considered as well. Relativists would argue that there is no possible "one size" that fits all the billions of people on Earth. Also, they argue that it is undeniable that society's values change over time; slavery is no longer acceptable, for example. Other examples would be the concept of polygamy and its evolution through the centuries, and the evolving question of same-sex marriage. What worldly and human things are permanent forever anyway? No wonder relativists are eager to replace the old virtues with new ones such as pluralism, diversity, otherness, dissimilarity, distinctiveness, heterogeneousness, differentiability, and the like.

Do "Wokeness" and "Cancel Culture" Cancel God?

Once upon a time, people used principles taken from holy books to accordingly live their lives. They used to refer to the sages and the saints as living examples of what they were supposed to think about right and wrong.

Once upon a time, people used to gather on a given territory, agree on certain rules and regulations, and write a constitution that citizens of that country abided by. Once upon a time, different groups from different parties and persuasions used to respect each other, listen to each other, and accommodate each other.

Once upon a time, there used to be some kind of collective and universal wisdom to abide by. No more. Personal experience took over and defined the terms of shaping reality and truth. Furthermore, pushing this new understanding to the extreme, some people wanted to decide for themselves if, for example, they were men, women, or no gender.

This is how it used to be until the day certain groups of people decided to abolish references, traditions, and outdated regulations and rules. How to do that? Activists, through the media, governments, corporations, institutions, colleges, and demonstrations, would fiercely move ahead in directly attacking religion and family. By doing so, they hope to destroy all the virtues and values that keep societies bonded, morally sound, healthy, and happy. The days of what we used to call virtues and values are over. Today, and especially in Western culture, traditional morals, ethics, and values are belittled, mocked, and attacked, and references to God are obliterated. We seem very close, if we are not already there, to the point where only one set of beliefs is allowed by those in control, and other points of view are silenced and banned.

Welcome to cancel culture. In cancel culture, power—not truth—is the way to change things. Power dictates truth. No wonder truth keeps changing. Power demands, and truth follows. "Do whatever I tell you, or else." Negotiations are meaningless. Only submission makes sense. Power is the fundamental force of social change.

Although cancel culture popped onto the scene in recent years, the idea goes far back to a time when there were two truths: your truth and my truth. It would be to your advantage to agree with my truth, and if you didn't, you ran the risk of being cancelled. Aren't wars throughout history an illustration of such an attitude?

On a daily basis, and instead of going to war every time we disagree with someone, we use other forms of cancel culture. We can cancel a person, celebrities, and groups of people, social media, and anyone who does not agree with us as a "well-deserved" punishment for their wrong opinions—because our opinions are the right ones. Tell me about biases! However, on many occasions, it is not only a question of biases; it is an agenda, a message, a mission to accomplish. We do this either violently sometimes, or non-violently most of the time. Here, the computer is always ready to help in targeting any person, any company, any institution, or any leader, from our comfortable rooms. Cancel culture activists would use ridicule, attempts to have bank accounts removed, get people fired, boycott companies and stores, and employ any manipulative means of attempting to control others.

Such a climate of wokeness and cancel culture has its consequences in society. A lack of shared truth causes erosion of trust, and society becomes divided and fragmented. Also, the fact that individuals have their own truth only leads to an uncertain and confused future because of the loss of a standard of what is right and what is wrong.

God, in this context, is not safe either. God, the creator and the ultimate authority of all things, can be cancelled. When people try to cancel a person, a group, or an institution on the grounds of their biased religious beliefs and fanaticism, they are, in practice, cancelling the supreme authority and replacing it with their own authority. In order to successfully reach the so-called "mission accomplished" goal, God must be cancelled. With God cancelled, civilization as we know it is cancelled too. Such a path of darkness and confusion will inevitably lead to the law of the jungle.

Part 2: Post Truth Reality

"There are two ways to be fooled. One is to believe what isn't true; the other is to refuse to believe what is true."

—Soren Kierkegaard

4| Liars Lie (1)

Liars look straight into others' eyes and boldly claim as true what they know, and most of their listeners also know, to be untrue. Truth still exists regardless of what liars say.

The Repeated Lie

"A lie told often enough becomes the truth" is believed to have been said by Vladimir Lenin. William James said something similar: "There's nothing so absurd that if you repeat it often enough, people will believe it." Indeed, in our ordinary lives, especially in matters of politics and culture, lies are so powerful that they may create reality.

Are we surprised if we see some people, especially among our leaders and politicians, lie to us almost constantly, persistently, and repeatedly? Are we surprised if we see a good number of them living a double life – one life for you and me, for the show and support, and the other for them to hide in the secrecy of evasiveness and darkness?

Here we should not generalise, though, because we still have, thank God, people who believe in integrity and honesty. However, it is fair to say that the majority of us have adopted the "politically correct" doctrine that allows the use of any means, honest or not, in order to reach a projected goal. Believe it or not, politics and religion seem to offer the most fertile ground for lies and bad behaviour.

Truth can be the first and most recognisable casualty of modern life. If we no longer know what a lie is, chances are that's because we no longer know what truth is. One of the most telling illustrations of this fact is our modern wars and how our corporate media's coverage describes the events. The old saying, "The first casualty of war is the truth," is true indeed. Do we really know why we went to this or that war? Do we really know who broke the ceasefire first? Do we really know how many people were killed on both sides? Do we really know who became very rich as a result of this or that conflict? Add to this all the other questions you may have in mind. But this we seem to certainly know and agree on: "The first casualty of war is the truth."

Apart from a few exceptions—thank God for these good exceptions—our conversations, behaviours, and relationships in general unfortunately do not inspire trust. How privileged and lucky you are if you can say you have never been lied to! Do you know anyone who has never been lied to? Personally, I have not met that person yet.

Truth is one of the first casualties of our modern life. The question "Is it true?" has become, it is sad to say, "Whose truth is it?" People tend to live by their beliefs, even if their beliefs are not true.

Most people usually shape their beliefs about life, the world, and others by what they see, hear, and read, without dismissing irrelevant information. Repetition is one of the ways of influencing those beliefs or even creating them. Repetition produces a certain manipulable climate of familiarization within us that allows us to be less critical of a proposition and more accepting of a situation. No wonder then, repetition has been adopted as a significant factor in altering beliefs, attitudes, or convictions—e.g. advertisements, propaganda, social values, political issues, etc. Repetition has the power to even create needs we don't really have and help us accept a lie as truth. Kate Mosse observed: "You well know that if a lie is repeated often enough, in the face of the clearest evidence to the contrary, even the most level-headed of men start to believe in it. Falsehood easily becomes accepted truth." John F. Kennedy also said: "No matter how big the lie; repeat it often enough and the masses will regard it as the truth." That is true. But what is also true is what Colum McCann remarked: "The repeated lies become history, but they don't necessarily become the truth."

When a Half-Truth Becomes One of the Most Effective Lies

Cambridge Dictionary defines a half-truth as "a statement that is intended to deceive by being only partly true." Even though a statement might be partly true and is presented as such, the hidden intention, knowingly or unknowingly, is to conceal the full truth by making something appear more plausible by exploiting ambiguous language that leads listeners to draw incorrect conclusions. That is the "art" of manipulating perception and public opinion without making false statements. It is the "art" of blending facts, ideologies, and omissions in a way that is designed to deceive, creating the intended confusion. Here are some indisputable examples of half-truths:

1. **"This candidate is the most experienced."** The official might be so, based on years in office. But it doesn't say much about the quality or relevance of that experience, and it completely omits mentioning the skills and accomplishments of other candidates.

2. **"Non-toxic products."** Non-toxic suggests safety. Therefore, one can use this non-toxic product as one wish. However, since consumers do not have more specific information about that product, they think the product is entirely harmless and without any side effects or potential long-term risks.
3. **"Clinically proven."** One would immediately think of a large scientific endorsement. Maybe not so. It could be the result of limited studies, non-independent research, or non-conclusive scientific results.
4. **"Most doctors recommend this medication."** This could be true. But it does not say that they use it for specific purposes and special circumstances, or that they recommend other medications as well. The purpose of the statement is to use professional endorsement to invite buyers to purchase the product without explaining the context.
5. **"Studies concluded."** This sounds great. One can certainly learn from science and experience. However, we should proceed with caution, because other studies may have concluded the opposite—or at least cast doubt on what the first studies concluded. It seems unbelievably difficult for human beings to ponder both sides of an issue. People seem to be more at ease with, and emotionally more comfortable by, aligning themselves with one side of an issue.
6. **"Knowing good and evil."** The serpent said: "You will not die; for God knows that when you eat of it your eyes will be opened, and you will be like God, knowing good and evil" (Genesis 3:4–5). Satan's ways are seductive and presented as a "win-win" choice. Eve's eyes were opened,

but her capacity for knowing good and evil was very far from being like God's. Humanity continues to be seduced by the half-truth of Satan's ways of thinking and behaving, when it should have chosen to see things with God's eyes.

7. **"All we need is love."** Of course, we do need love. Who can deny this simple and obvious truth? Jesus said: "You shall love the Lord your God with all your heart, and with all your soul, and with your entire mind…. You shall love your neighbour as yourself" (Matthew 22:37, 39). However, and while remaining central in our relationship with God and others, love should not be just feeling and good sentiment. Love should be action also; otherwise, love becomes a half-truth. Saint John tells us: "Little children, let us love, not in word or speech, but in truth and action" (1 John 3:18). Also, the famous chapter to the Corinthians by Saint Paul is so telling. It says:
   1. Though I speak with
   the tongues of men and of angels, and have not charity, I am become as sounding brass, or a tinkling cymbal.
   2. And though I have the gift
   of prophecy, and understand all mysteries, and all knowl edge; and though I have all faith, so that I
   could remove mountains, and have not charity, I am noth ing.
   3. And though I bestow all my goods to feed the
   poor, and though I give my body to be burned, and have not charity, it profiteth me nothing.
   4. Charity suffereth long, and
   is kind; charity envieth not; charity vaunteth not itself, is not puffed up,

5. Doth not behave
itself unseemly, seeketh not her own, is not easily
provoked, thinketh no evil;
6. Rejoiceth not in iniquity, but rejoiceth in the truth;
7. Beareth all things, believeth all things, hopeth all things,
endureth all things.
8. Charity never faileth: but whether there
be prophecies, they shall fail; whether there
be tongues, they shall cease; whether there
be knowledge, it shall vanish away.
9. For we know in part, and we prophesy in part.
10. But when that which is perfect is come, then that which
is in part shall be done away.
11. When I was a child, I spake as a child, I understood as a
child, I thought as a child: but when I became a man, I
put away childish things.
12. For now we see through a glass, darkly;
but then face to face: now I know in part; but then shall
I know even as also I am known.
13. And now abideth faith, hope, charity, these three; but the
greatest of these is charity. (1 Corinthians 13 KJV)

8. "I am here to reform the Church, the nation, the system, and not to destroy them," a leader would say. No leader wants to destroy, but in a very subtle way, a leader can spread confusion, ambiguity, double talk, and recruit corrupt people who can corrupt and destroy. Originally, although that leader's intention was to reform, the results of the actions taken were a subtle destruction. It is also a half-truth when one sets a goal and, at the same time, uses what it takes to avoid reaching that goal.

9. The eloquent rhetoric and the complicit silence. When facing a difficult situation—a war, for example—a leader would make a beautiful speech on the importance of peace while providing what is necessary to pursue the war. Another leader may choose complicit silence while not doing anything to stop the killing. Half-truths—good speeches and complicit silence—may be used as means for spreading more evil on the earth. We skillfully do this, whether intentionally or unintentionally.

Such examples, and many more similar ones taken from any life situation, show that human beings find it extremely difficult to tell the whole truth, even if they say they are telling the truth, the whole truth, and nothing but the truth. People are inclined to always tell half-truths, even when they are not aware of doing so. We should always remember that half-truths are not the truth. "Half the truth is often a great lie," said Benjamin Franklin, and for Mark Twain, "A half-truth is the most cowardly of lies."

Also, our reality shows us that half-truths surround us from all sides. In any facet of life, we always encounter statements intended to mislead, manipulate, deceive, and create the illusion of honesty and integrity. Half-truths rely on ambiguity, exaggeration, and information or omission to manipulate perceptions. The venomous deception hides within the mixture of accuracy and inaccuracy, truth and falsehood, and facts and fantasies.

In the labyrinth of modern life at all its levels—individual, social, political, national, international, religious, and especially when it comes to careers and business—half-truths seem to serve as the common currency of choice for the majority of activists, and this makes the line between persuasion and deception blurry and foggy. This is the subtle art of manipulating facts to present an image far rosier than what reality is. This strategy counts on the ambiguity of language, relying deeply on the complexity of human psychology.

Half-truth practices break trust, demonstrate disrespect, deracinate integrity, exploit others' naiveté, and deprive others of their right to make informed decisions based on obvious facts.

The Trojan horse Stratagem

The story of the Trojan Horse is one of the most well-known tales of ancient Greek mythology. The story is about a conflict that took place around the 12th or 13th century BC between the Greeks and the city of Troy. To end this war that lasted about 10 years, as it was believed, the Greeks pretended to withdraw, leaving behind a huge wooden horse with a group of warriors concealed inside. When the Trojans brought the horse into their city to celebrate their victory, the Greek soldiers, once inside Troy, climbed out of the horse, opened the city gates to their comrades, and the city was sacked and the population slaughtered or enslaved.

What does the Trojan Horse symbolize?

The Trojan Horse, which was a symbol of the deceit and trickery used by the Greeks to defeat the enemy, the Trojans, became over the centuries a powerful symbol of cunning and subterfuge in literature, art, culture, and daily life connections at all levels. Then it became a symbol of the alarm against favours or gifts offered by others, as they may not be as "innocent" favours or gifts as one would think they appear to be. It describes, in essence, how something that seems innocent, friendly, and generous can be used to infiltrate enemy lines. The world is not always what it seems to be, indeed.

People do things for a reason, and that reason is often centred on self-interest. The Trojan Horse became a metaphor for hidden agendas and concealed intentions that lie beneath the surface. It shows us the necessity of taking a closer look at what we are dealing with and not accepting things at face value. It is an invitation for caution and scrutiny in the face of potential deception and hidden lies. It is a great reminder of the existence of hidden agendas, deceit, and betrayal that we should not ignore.

The Trojan Horse tale may find its palpable application in politics more than in any other field of human endeavour. How often do we see seemingly benign proposals that may carry ulterior motives and hidden dangers? How often do we see legislative proposals, alternative programmes, and policy recommendations that, while appearing beneficial on the surface, have in reality the potential to undermine existing principles and values, as well as systems and institutions? How many times do we see plans that seem harmless on the surface, but in reality, carry seeds of devastation and destruction?

Here, one cannot fail to mention the fact that "Trojan", in modern times, has jumped into computer technology. Cyber news explains it this way: "Trojan (also known as Trojan horse) are a common kind of malicious program. By pretending to be a legitimate program or file, the malicious code is easy to install unknowingly. While every Trojan pretends to be another kind of program, they can do anything, from stealing your banking information to encrypting your files and demanding a ransom."

5 | Liars Lie (2)

Lies come sometimes unequivocal, clear-cut, and hard and fast. Sometimes, they take more nuanced, subtle, and serpentine roads. Liars may sometimes be aware of what they are doing and, very often, they are not even aware of what they are doing.

The Lies We Believe

Our mind is the constant companion in our life journey. It lives with us day and night. It tells us stories all the time. Some of these stories are true, but many—probably the majority of them—are lies, and, consciously or unconsciously, we believe them. They play in our heads like a tape recorder. When we listen to them long enough, they give us the feeling that they are true, even though they are really lies. The longer these tapes have been played, the more we believe they are true, when they are living lies. Those lies are the beliefs, assumptions, perspectives, attitudes, or expectations that don't fit reality. We don't look for them. They are already there. They came from a variety of sources—parents, friends, schools, culture, social, political, and religious environments—and all that is preventing us from seeing our authentic self and ultimate destiny. Although these sources contribute greatly to our formation and growth toward a fulfilled life, they may carry, at the same time, seeds of deception and duplicity. A few examples of the lies we believe would bring light to those areas of our lives we usually like to keep unexamined:

1. "I can't feel good about myself, unless everyone loves me, accepts me, and approves my way." This is the life of a social chameleon that needs to change colour in order to fit every situation and keep everyone happy. "Pleasers" are not genuine people. They lie to others and especially to themselves by losing the sense of their true identity. One can see the danger of giving power over you to others—friends, family members, co-workers, and others. We may lose ourselves if we continuously attempt to gain everyone's love and approval. The truth is that some people are not going to like us no matter how hard we try to please them.
2. "I am happy only when things go my way." This is not a recipe for happiness, but for unhappiness. Reality is not under our control. Gorgeous weather does not come when we desire it to come, traffic lights don't change when we want them to, our candidates for office don't always win when we want them to win, and the life ticket we buy or work for is not necessarily the winning ticket. Let us stop this subtle lie and admit that we can still enjoy the day even though it did not come as we wished it to be, and we can be content in spite of not having the world go our way.
3. "It is always the other's fault." We often tend not to take responsibility for our actions, as if what happens to us is somebody else's fault. If we don't reach our goals, it is because others were in our way. The "Look what they do to us" victim attitude is a lie that helps us justify our denial of responsibility.
4. "I can have it all." Really? How? Look at Solomon, the wealthiest and wisest man on the earth during his life,

and how he concluded. He said: "The lover of the money will not be satisfied with money; nor the lover of wealth, with gain. This is also vanity" (Ecclesiastes 5:10). He also said: "I saw all the deeds that are done under the sun; and see, all is vanity and a chasing after wind" (Ecclesiastes 1:14). Dissatisfaction is the result of the "one can have it all" lie. A simple psychological truth teaches us that the more we have or expect to have, the less the results will satisfy us.

5. "Just be like me." That is the "I am the measure for every good thing" lie. Certain individuals arrogantly think that they are privileged by having the best values, the best principles, the best lifestyle, and that everyone should imitate them. The truth is that no one should be a carbon copy of someone else. We were born with unique personalities, talents, and characteristics. Thank God we are not all the same. It would have been boring.
6. "In order for God to use me, I am supposed to be spiritually strong." It is our arrogance that is the reason underlying such a lie. The truth is that it is not the healthy who need a doctor, but the sick and weak. Through our weaknesses, God can show power. St. Paul reminds us, "For whenever I am weak, then I am strong" (2 Corinthians 12:10).
7. "Distortion truths." Knowingly or unknowingly, we often overgeneralise, reason and argue emotionally, think in the abstract, polarise, take things personally, victimise, or magnify and exaggerate. There is always, it seems, a kind of subjective touch in what we think and do. To say it more bluntly, we may need to ask

ourselves whether or not we are able, from a human point of view, to ever state an objective truth. St. Paul's prescription indicates a different path. It says: "Do not be conformed to the world, but be transformed by the renewing of your minds, so that you may discern what is the will of God—what is good and acceptable and perfect" (Romans 12:2).

Our Human "Isms"

Our mind wants to understand everything, and that includes what it cannot understand God. God is understood by faith, and faith is beyond what is rational; it is a grace. Throughout the centuries, the mind has kept trying to understand and explain the known, the unknown, and the unknowable. We seem to continue in the same way again and again, believing that the "isms" we have created may provide us with the right answer. They did not. They do not.

Let us browse through some of the "isms" that we thought might have the solution we were eagerly looking for, but we either found a dissatisfying answer or found no answer at all.

Agnosticism

If theists profess confidence in their views with regard to the existence of God, and if atheists want to prove absolutely the non-existence of God, agnostics throughout the centuries have held the middle ground of not knowing whether or not God exists. For them, evidence for God's existence is balanced by evidence against God's existence. Because of the limitations of the human intellect, they prefer not to form a final judgement as to whether or not God exists.

Atheism

Atheism, generally speaking, is the absence of belief in God's existence. Some atheists find themselves practically in the categories of scepticism, indifference, or just ignorance. However, some others have gone further. For these, it is not a question of belief only; it is a question of hope that there is no God because they don't want to deal even with the idea that maybe there is a God. C.S. Lewis, among many others, noted the irony of the atheists' position by saying that "atheists express their rage against God although in their view He does not exist."

Deism

Deism believes in God, but as a religious practice based on reason only. It does not accept supernatural revelations of any sort. God does not intervene in the universe; God leaves the universe to run by its own laws. This is a religion without revelation that exemplifies the vast confidence in reason. Deists believe that the study of Nature and the use of reason are more helpful in understanding God than any scriptures, creeds, or traditions. Rousseau and Voltaire in France, and Benjamin Franklin and Thomas Jefferson in the USA, are among those who professed such beliefs.

Fundamentalism

Applied to religions, fundamentalism is the belief that the absolute and infallible truth is found only in the inviolable "word" of God that is read literally in every word of a holy book and practised in a sacred tradition. Such a belief has the capacity to affect deeply – and it does – the very structure of society and to become the dominant and conclusive factor in political systems.

Existentialism

Existentialism insists on being, and being cannot be the subject of objective enquiry. Therefore, existence should be understood through a personal experience of feeling, thinking, suffering... with the will to make our own choices. If, for Kierkegaard, who is usually considered the originator of existentialism, God gives meaning to life, for Sartre, who took Nietzsche's "God is dead" message to heart, the only resource is our freedom to choose the way we want to see the world and live in the world.

Fideism

For fideism, the essential religious doctrines cannot be established and proved by rational means. They must be accepted by faith. Faith is the only valid authority because religious experience is beyond the limits of reason and human comprehension. The finite mind cannot grasp the infinite and the unimaginable. The non-believers have used the principle of "faith alone" as a "good" reason to justify their doubts.

Jihadism

Jihadism is often defined as "holy war," but not all jihads involve combat. Personal jihad suggests the effort to be righteous and to purge one's soul of sin and worldly desires. Jihad also refers to both defensive and offensive warfare against the enemies of Islam, the infidels, and those who practise a religion that is moderate, tolerant, and secularised. At the present time, and because of some extremist groups, jihad tends to mean – wrongly – terrorism. In fact, authentic Islam, with the Sharia (Muslim law), forbids the slaughter of women, children, and non-combatants.

Manichaeism

Manichaeism was an influential religious movement founded and spread by Mani, the Persian prophet. It taught a radical dualism of good and evil, light and darkness, God and matter. For the Manichaeans, the way to return to the divine source is through severe asceticism. Before his conversion to Christianity, St Augustine was an adherent of this movement.

Materialism

Materialism is the theory that says that whatever exists is matter or is dependent on matter. Therefore, notions such as "mind," "spirit," and "God" should be rejected. But what is matter? Philosophically speaking, materialism was ill-defined; it became like a certain policy or a way of seeing the world rather than a "real" reality. We still need a clear definition of what materialism is.

Modernism

Modernism believes in the ability of the mind to attain truth. It does so through reason, reflection, observation, scientific methods, discovery, and technological advances. Many modernists assume that human dignity, morality, freedom, and progress can be preserved and fostered by reason and human potential without reference to God. Reason, not God, is the starting point for understanding and living.

Monism

For monism, everything is reducible to a single substance because of the basic oneness of being – one essence, principle, or energy. In fact, all the differences between beings are not real but illusion. Monism is closely associated with pantheism, which believes that God is either, or indwells, everything. Basically, there is no difference between Creator and creation. God is the "life-principle" and "all is one."

Monotheism

Monotheism is the belief that there is but one God. This God is usually given the attributes of omnipotence, omnipresence, and omniscience. This God, who is the source of morality and redemption, is intimately involved with our spiritual and physical worlds. Judaism, Christianity, and Islam are monotheistic.

Naturalism

Naturalism claims that the universe is self-existent and self-explanatory, and it operates according to natural laws. There is no need for any explanation that goes beyond the physical phenomena and the observable. Therefore, it rejects religion, mysticism, magic, Platonic forms, and supernatural beings. It was attributed to Emile Zola for saying, "Civilization will not attain to its perfection until the last stone from the last church falls on the last priest."

Nihilism

For nihilism, there is no point or meaning to life or the universe. Therefore, all forms of morality are false and impossible, all values are baseless, and God is dead in the first place. Nothing can really be known with absolute certainty. Nothing can be communicated successfully. It is the reign of radical scepticism, absurdity, and anarchy.

Pantheism

Pantheism is the doctrine that teaches that everything is God and God is everything. This is the "All-god-ism" belief, one can say. Human beings, nature, and everything that exists constitute modes or elements of God's being. Every element of the universe is divine, and the divine is equally present in everything. God is not a distinct being in the sense of classical theism. The philosophy of Spinoza, in the West, is regarded as the classic example of this doctrine; Spinoza's God is not personal and not separate from the universe. The infinite substance is God and all things are "in" God.

Polytheism

Polytheism is the belief in the existence of many gods, as opposed to monotheism, which believes in the existence of one God. These gods are usually associated with different aspects of nature such as the sea, the earth, fire, wind, storms, etc. Other gods are associated with aspects of life such as fertility, motherhood, death, and rites of passage.

Postmodernism

Postmodernism excludes not only God, but also rationality as a foundation for making sense of reality and human experience. In fact, there is no universal truth, there is no universal morality, and there is no universal certainty of anything. Postmodernism is sceptical (or suspicious) of big systems and critical of views that claim to be rational, unbiased, or neutral. It rather believes that our ideas and judgements are always formed within a historical-cultural context. There are no absolute truths, no absolute values, and no absolute religious or ethical laws. There is no objectivity in anything. There is only subjectivity.

Rationalism

For rationalism, everything is explicable by "reason alone"—the world is organised in such a way that truths can be deduced by pure reason, and what we learn rationally is the real world. Therefore, religious beliefs are not taken seriously because they are irrational. Other sources of knowledge such as faith, custom, superstition, and the like are rejected. Some rationalists think that God enables human beings to know the truth and the existence of God by means of reason, but most rationalists are atheists or agnostics. Rationalism wants and encourages people to think for themselves.

Relativism

Relativism sees that all truths are subjective. It maintains that ideas are the product of language, history, and cultural conventions. Therefore, they are denied any objective and universal standards. Furthermore, relativists see in relativism a sign of maturity; the "immature" society and religion rely on inviolable creeds and dogmas to ensure stability, but the "mature" society and relativism know how to accept responsibility for the differences of opinion and action. Here, it seems necessary and adequate to quote what Cardinal Ratzinger (who became Pope Benedict XVI) famously said in his homily of April 18, 2005. Contrasting a steadfast faith in Christ and Church with a pernicious pluralism, he said:

> How many winds of doctrine have we known in recent decades, how many ideological currents, how many ways of thinking? The small boat of the thought of many Christians has often been tossed about by these waves – flung from one extreme to another: from Marxism to liberalism, even to libertinism; from collectivism to radical individualism; from atheism to a vague religious mysticism; from agnosticism to syncretism and so forth. Every day new sects spring up, and what St. Paul says about human deception and the trickery that strives to entice people into error (cf. Eph 4:14) comes true. Today, having a clear faith based on the Creed of the Church is often labelled as fundamentalism. Whereas relativism, that is, letting oneself be "tossed here and there, carried about by every wind of doctrine", seems the only attitude that can cope with modern times. We are building a dictatorship of relativism that does not

recognise anything as definitive and whose ultimate goal consists solely of one's own ego and desires.

We, however, have a different goal: the Son of God, the true man. He is the measure of true humanism. An "adult" faith is not a faith that follows the trends of fashion and the latest novelty; a mature adult faith is deeply rooted in friendship with Christ. It is this friendship that opens us up to all that is good and gives us a criterion by which to distinguish the true from the false, and deceit from truth.

(Cappella Papale – Mass "Pro Eligendo Romano Pontifice" – Homily of His Eminence Card. Joseph Ratzinger, Dean of the College of Cardinals, Vatican Basilica – Monday 18 April 2005)

Secularism

Secularism denies any control or influence of religious beliefs on modern societies. Therefore, religious perceptions, values, and terms of reference can no longer run a life that should be based on the development of scientific and cultural ideas. Even though it is not necessarily anti-religious, secularism means in practice, among other things: the end of religious teaching in State-funded education, the repeal of the laws that were designed to protect religiously defined values, the exclusion of religious criteria in appointments for public offices or in the application of civil rights, the denial—maybe not in theory, but certainly in practice—of the right of religious liberty, etc.

Theism

Theism believes in God rather than in a god. This God is the creator of the universe. God sustains the universe and intervenes within it in natural and non-natural ways. God is the primary cause of all that was, is, and will be. God is personal, omnipotent, omniscient, and omnipresent in the creation but distinct from it. Judaism, Christianity, and Islam can be considered the three major theistic religions.

Transhumanism

Wikipedia explains:

> Transhumanism (abbreviated as H+ or h+) is an international cultural and intellectual movement with an eventual goal of fundamentally transforming the human condition by developing and making widely available technologies to greatly enhance human intellectual, physical, and psychological capacities. Transhumanist thinkers study the potential benefits and dangers of emerging technologies that could overcome fundamental human limitations, as well as the ethics of developing and using such technologies. The most common thesis put forward is that human beings may eventually be able to transform themselves into beings with such greatly expanded abilities as to merit the label posthuman.

This means that we can now control our own evolution and fundamentally transform our human condition. Indeed, our developing technologies will help us to greatly enhance our physical, intellectual, and psychological capacities. This evolution will lengthen human life and enable everyone to enjoy better minds and bodies. Moreover, this means that, by trying to play the Creator, we are trying to control everything, including our human nature, and we do this by taking God's place. This way, when "God does not exist" or when "God is dead," we won't have a definition for our human nature, as Jean-Paul Sartre claimed. He said that "There is no human nature, since there is no god to conceive it." Consequently, it will be up to us to define our human nature as we want, and to choose our own life purposes as we wish. Such a liberty, without a definition of human nature, one must conclude, is founded on an atheistic ground.

All these "isms" that are mentioned here—many other "isms" could have been mentioned also—lead to the conclusion that humans are trying by any means to make themselves God. The reality is that the way God is conceived, so is conceived our outlook on life. The "religious" outlook is at the core of our culture, politics, economics, values, and the way we think, act, and live.

If we think that our "isms" are always innocent and straightforward, we should think again and reconsider what we thought was an honest conviction. Beware of the disguised and hidden duplicity, whether we are aware of it or not.

Why Do We Lie?

In the thesauruses, we see the word "lie" synonymous with falsehood, untruth, delusion, perjury, duplicity, insincerity, deceitfulness, phoniness, fallaciousness, simulation, hypocrisy, dishonesty, prevarication, distortion, fabrication, false pretence, sham, and more. This is more than enough to convince us about the extent and forms of lies we, consciously or unconsciously, can be guilty of in our daily lives.

A few years ago, authors James Paterson and Peter Kim conducted an interesting survey, which went beyond the superficial five-minute poll, about private morals and values.

This study was published in a book called *The Day America Told the Truth*. What they found is astonishing. For example:

> Lying has become an integral part of the American culture, a trait of the American character. We lie and don't even think about it. We lie for no reason. The writer Vance Bourjaily once said, "Like most men, I tell a hundred lies a day." That's about right. And the people we lie to most are those closest to us.

Just about everyone lies—91 percent of us lie regularly.

> Americans are making up their own rules, their own laws. In effect, we're all making up our own moral codes. Only13 percent of us believe in all of the Ten Commandments. Forty percent of us believe in five of the Ten Commandments. We choose which laws of God we believe in. There is absolutely no moral consensus in this country as there was in the 1950s, when all our institutions commanded more respect. Today, there is very little respect for the law—for any kind of law.
>
> Yesterday's verities had vanished. Unpredictability and chaos became the norm.

If these findings are true, and if what a TV preacher once said, "The average person lies about 200 times a day," is true, we do not have a pretty picture of ourselves at all. Isn't this the picture of an ethical disarray—a jungle?

The problem of lying is obviously not the monopoly of one special country, or one special culture, or one special ethnic group, or one special religion, or one special time in history. Look, for example, how philosopher Simone Weil (1909–1943) warned her fellow citizens in France: "We live in an age so impregnated with lies that even the virtue of blood voluntarily sacrificed is insufficient to put us back on path of truth."

St. Paul wrote to the Colossians, "Do not lie to one another" (Colossians 3:9). Aristotle warned, "All that one gains by falsehood is not to be believed when he speaks the truth."

Why in the world do we seem to have difficulty telling the truth? Here we do not have a shortage of reasons.

A first reason is that we might be guilty of a bigger failure and want to hide it. Lying, which we consider a lesser evil, becomes a way of self-protection. Therefore, we lie for security reasons.

A second reason is the reason of character. When lies become habits, they also become character. It does not take long to be known as a chronic liar, in which case we lose hold of the truth by believing our own lies. Also, sometimes we lie because we can lie for the fun of it, and to get away with it and not be caught. Fyodor Dostoevsky (1821–1881) wrote:

> When we lie to ourselves, and believe our own lies, we become unable to recognize truth, either in ourselves or in anyone else, and we end up losing respect for ourselves and for others. When we have no respect for anyone, we can no longer love, and, in order to divert ourselves, having no love in us, we yield to our impulses, indulge in the lowest forms of pleasure, and behave in the end like

an animal, in satisfying our vices. And it all comes from lying—lying to others and ourselves.

A third reason is that repeated lies, which give the appearance of success, help liars become more accomplished in the "craft" of lying. They become experts in lying.

A fourth reason is that we can, in order to justify our conduct, rationalise and give explanations for any behaviour we choose, even though in our hearts we do not believe what we are saying. One obvious justification for our conduct, we think, is the use of polls and statistics. "80 percent do this or that," we say. But we forget that truth has nothing to do with majority, minority, or even unanimity. This is not its language. The Earth was revolving around the Sun even when we were saying the opposite.

A fifth reason is that by substituting living the lie for living in the truth, we not only turn any sense of morality upside down, but we think that it is our job—a proof of loyalty—to do this for the good of the company or administration we work for. In this sense, we think that lies pay or promise to pay.

Loyalty to a company, a community, or a country should never blind us to the truth. Even though loyalty is certainly a wonderful quality, we should seek truth first, because loyalty can cover many sins and crimes. Dorothy Day rightly pointed out: "Our job is not to look for results but to be faithful to the truth." Therefore, results should flow from the truth, not the truth from results.

Furthermore, we are always tempted to adapt and adjust facts to what our superiors would like to see and hear, and we turn, as they do, a blind eye to what they do not want to see.

Some of us are becoming so skilled in lying that we are no longer "amateurs," but real "professionals."

Obviously, certain careers, more than others, count heavily on such skills. A sixth reason is to set unrealistic goals and unreachable ideals for oneself. These goals and ideals can certainly be good in themselves, but they can also constitute an effective tactic of falsehood when we set them so high that they cannot be reached.

A seventh reason is that, in order to advance an ideology or a certain agenda of any kind, we tend to create a persona for ourselves. The Latin word "persona" means "a mask." We want to wear a mask and act differently from who and what we are, in an effort to improve ourselves. Our world, which counts heavily on first impressions, encourages us to "sell ourselves on sight." In such a world, depth becomes less important than appearance, honesty less significant than "face value," and truth less attractive than winning lies. This is why we do not hesitate to go to plastic surgeons, implant hair, spin résumés, twist events, and over-inflate our capacities. Such makeovers are seen today as a normal road to advancement in life, rather than a handicap.

An eighth reason is that we may wear a mask for latent motives. Maybe there is some part (perhaps the deepest part) of ourselves that we would rather not reveal openly, or perhaps we fear confronting ourselves. Maybe we are not sure what it is either. Our unconscious can be a warehouse for repressed truths we have difficulty facing. In this context, Plato talked about Appetite, Freud about the Id, Nietzsche about Dionysus, and Jung about the Shadow. Is it not Socrates' intent for us to get rid of the mask we wear and reveal ourselves, at least to ourselves? His famous dictum "Know thyself," from about 2400 years ago, is more needed than ever in modern times. We do not love ourselves, and we do not know that we do not love ourselves. It seems that no matter what we do, it is not enough. A lie, we think, can cover up this deep, empty hole of dissatisfaction and the need to be loved. A lie may attract attention to us—the attention we desperately seek. We need to know the truth about ourselves, but we don't.

6 | Liars' Ways (1)

There are multiple ways liars use to spread lies. Some of these ways are blatant and palpable, while others are subtle and crafty. Let us review some of these methods.

The "Serpent" Way

Since the beginning of time, the question, "Did God say…?" that the serpent asked the woman in the book of Genesis, has remained a thought-provoking and intriguing question throughout the centuries. It still is. The story of that event is rich in detail and should be read in its entirety and attentively. Here is the story as it is told in the Bible.

1. Now the serpent was more subtle than any beast of the field which the LORD God had made. And he said unto the woman, Yea, hath God said, Ye shall not eat of every tree of the garden?
2. And the woman said unto the serpent, We may eat of the fruit of the trees of the garden:
3. But of the fruit of the tree which *is* in the midst of the garden, God hath said, Ye shall not eat of it, neither shall ye touch it, lest ye die.
4. And the serpent said unto the woman, Ye shall not surely die:

5. For God doth know that in the day ye eat thereof, then your eyes shall be opened, and ye shall be as gods, knowing good and evil.
6. And when the woman saw that the tree *was* good for food, and that it *was* pleasant to the eyes, and a tree to be desired to make *one* wise, she took of the fruit thereof, and did eat, and gave also unto her husband with her; and he did eat.
7. And the eyes of them both were opened, and they knew that they *were* naked; and they sewed fig leaves together, and made themselves aprons.
8. And they heard the voice of the LORD God walking in the garden in the cool of the day: and Adam and his wife hid themselves from the presence of the LORD God amongst the trees of the garden.
9. And the LORD God called unto Adam, and said unto him, Where *art* thou?
10. And he said, I heard thy voice in the garden, and I was afraid, because I *was* naked; and I hid myself.
11. And he said, Who told thee that thou *wast* naked? Hast thou eaten of the tree, whereof I commanded thee that thou shouldest not eat?
12. And the man said, The woman whom thou gavest *to be* with me, she gave me of the tree, and I did eat.
13. And the LORD God said unto the woman, What *is* this *that* thou hast done? And the woman said, The serpent beguiled me, and I did eat.
14. And the LORD God said unto the serpent, Because thou hast done this, thou *art* cursed above all cattle, and above every beast of the field; upon thy belly shalt thou go, and dust shalt thou eat all the days of thy life.

15. And I will put enmity between thee and the woman, and between thy seed and her seed; it shall bruise thy head, and thou shalt bruise his heel.
16. Unto the woman he said, I will greatly multiply thy sorrow and thy conception; in sorrow thou shalt bring forth children; and thy desire *shall be* to thy husband, and he shall rule over thee.
17. And unto Adam he said, Because thou hast hearkened unto the voice of thy wife, and hast eaten of the tree, of which I commanded thee, saying, Thou shalt not eat of it: cursed *is* the ground for thy sake; in sorrow shalt thou eat *of* it all the days of thy life;
18. Thorns also and thistles shall it bring forth to thee; and thou shalt eat the herb of the field;
19. In the sweat of thy face shalt thou eat bread, till thou return unto the ground; for out of it wast thou taken: for dust thou *art*, and unto dust shalt thou return.
20. And Adam called his wife's name Eve; because she was the mother of all living.
21. Unto Adam also and to his wife did the LORD God make coats of skins, and clothed them.
22. And the LORD God said, Behold, the man is become as one of us, to know good and evil: and now, lest he put forth his hand, and take also of the tree of life, and eat, and live for ever:
23. Therefore the LORD God sent him forth from the garden of Eden, to till the ground from whence he was taken.
24. So he drove out the man; and he placed at the east of the garden of Eden Cherubims, and a flaming sword

> which turned every way, to keep the way of the tree of life. (Genesis 3:1-24 KJV)

This story, in truth, can be considered the art of turning truth into a lie. St. John equates the serpent with Satan (see Revelation 12:9), and Jesus declares Satan to be the father of lies, and that there is no truth in him (see John 8:44). The venomous deception is not in what the serpent said, but in what it did not say. The intention is to undermine Eve's trust in God's goodness toward her. And this is what it did. It succeeded in injecting into Eve's mind the possibility of questioning God: What is God hiding from us? Why doesn't God want us to know good and evil? Is God afraid of us if we become powerful like him? Does becoming like him scare him? This temptation was appealing to Eve—representing the human condition—and she decided to know more, to be independent, and to decide for herself what is good and what is evil. It was all about power and vanity. Cleverly and skilfully, the serpent presented the advice in a way that sounded like the truth. That is the way good liars lie: by making what is questionable and false sound like it could be true.

Boom! Mission accomplished. It was a tour de force from the serpent. As was the case with Eve, we have continued throughout time, space, culture, and history to question God's ways, pretending to know what is better for us. As it was with Eve, so it is with us—we are easily deceived. None of us, no matter how powerful, intelligent, and successful we are, will ever really be "as God." Albert Einstein's famous line comes to mind here. He rightly said: "The more I learn, the more I realize how much I don't know." Indeed, our perspectives are tilted, slanted, biased, distorted, pretentious, arrogant, and unbalanced. We certainly are better off when we resist the voice of the serpent and stop questioning and challenging God's order.

The "Pharisee" Way

The "Woe to you, scribes and Pharisees, hypocrites!..." (Matthew 23:13) of Jesus continues to reverberate through time and space.

Almost daily, reports of hypocrisy find their way into the prime-time news. Respected leaders in the community are found guilty of financial fraud or sexual misconduct. Admired sports or entertainment personalities are caught with drug possession or domestic violence. Honourable high-profile figures are discovered to be living a double life.

What is wrong with us? Why do we have trouble with authenticity? What has happened to what used to be called "authenticity," "honesty," or "integrity"?

OK! Everyone, as reality shows, has one thing or another to sell. Everyone tries to persuade others to accept his or her ideas because he or she claims to know what is true and what is not. However, real life remains, by far, more persuasive.

This is precisely what hypocrisy is all about—the failure to practise what one preaches. One says something and does something else.

In religion as well as in the world in general, we constantly have to deal with hypocrites. Hypocrites are going to be among us as long as there is sin.

It is not uncommon for us to fail to walk the talk by not living what we preach. St. Paul—even St. Paul!—complained about this. He wrote: "I do not do the good I want, but the evil

I do not want is what I do. Now if I do what I do not want, it is no longer I that do it, but sin that dwells within me" (Romans 7:19–20).

Almost daily, we read and hear reports on hypocrisy. Under the umbrella of goodness, charitable works, and all kinds of services to others, we are, at the same time, shocked by the committed fraud, sexual abuses, and other crimes and lies.

No wonder people are becoming more and more cautious and less and less trusting. Where are the days when doors of homes and cars were kept unlocked, and where are the days when people's given word was more binding than written contracts?

No wonder many people are becoming more selective in their relationships. Many now seem to live by the conclusion, "Fool me once, shame on you; fool me twice, shame on me," or by the German proverb, "When the fox preaches, look to your geese."

It is strange and puzzling to see how we have become so addicted to untruth, how the discrepancy between one's actions and one's beliefs and convictions is ever expanding, and how we do too little to bring a remedy to such a disorder. We do not seem eager to do so, because hypocrisy may provide us with some social benefits.

If dictators or rich, influential individuals associate themselves with, let's say, a highly respected member of the clergy—by building a hospital, school, or orphanage, for example—those persons, without a doubt, would have done something positive for their communities, even if their "righteousness" was simply a means to hide what they did not want to show. Also, one can affect others by a kind of preaching that is not necessarily practised by the preacher, provided that the eloquent and charismatic preacher is not caught for not walking the talk. Even an atheist can, for example, preach the commandment of not stealing to his servants or employees, because this commandment works in his or her favour. This atheist can steal from others, but others cannot steal from him or her, and this is done in the name of "morality."

Virtues are not only spiritual realities; their social pragmatic side—good or suspicious—cannot be ignored. Even during conflicts, this is evident. It seems so charitable—and this is beautiful and highly recommended—to bring necessary aid to the victims of conflict and to the millions of displaced people as a result of war. But it would have been more charitable if we had worked to avoid the conflict in the first place. What is worse is when we provide weapons to this side or that side—or even to both sides—while we are sending aid to the victims. Doesn't such an attitude smell of hypocrisy?

Furthermore, can the Christian message still be taken seriously if Christians are not better than anyone else? Why should the general population listen to them, when obvious inconsistencies exist in their own house? Should the hypocrisy of some believers be considered the fruit of faith in Christ, or rather the violation of it? Should we identify the messenger with the message? Can we?

To this, St. Jerome (342–420) responds: "It is no fault of Christianity that a hypocrite falls into sin." Christians are called to live a life "worthy of the gospel of Christ" (Philippians 1:27). If they don't, that is because of sin, not because of the message. It would be a monumental error to identify Jesus' message with the way some of us live our lives.

When someone points the finger at a hypocrite believer to justify his or her own non-belief, he or she usually does this as an excuse for his or her own conduct. Jesus would say to them: "Do whatever they teach you and follow it; but do not do as they do, for they do not practise what they teach" (Matthew 23:3).

Jesus was unbelievably severe *vis-à-vis* the hypocrites of his time. He confronted them with harsh words:

> Woe to you, scribes and Pharisees, hypocrites!... Blind guides… blind fools… how blind you are!... You are like whitewashed tombs, which on the outside look beautiful, but inside they are full of the bones of the dead and of all kinds of filth. So you also on the outside look righteous to others, but inside you are full of hypocrisy and lawlessness…. You snakes, you brood of vipers! How can you escape being sentenced to hell? (Matthew 23:13-33)

Jesus wanted his followers to align themselves with the truth:

> Let your word be 'Yes, Yes' or 'No, No'; anything more than this come from the evil one. (Matthew 5:37)
> You will know the truth, and the truth will make you free. (John 8:32)

> I came to the world, to testify to the truth. Everyone who belongs to the truth listens to my voice. (John 18:37)

> I am the way, and the truth, and the life. (John 14:6)

> Those who do what is true come to the light, so that it may be clearly seen that their deeds have been done in God. (John 3:21)

> When the Spirit of truth comes, he will guide you into all the truth. (John 16:13)

John, Paul, and James echoed what Jesus said. They wrote:

> Grace and truth come through Jesus Christ. (John 1:17)

> I have no greater joy than this, to hear that my children are walking in the truth. (3 John 4)

> Fasten the belt of truth around your waist and put on the breastplate of righteousness. (Ephesians 6:14)
>
> Surely you have heard about him and were taught in him, as truth is in Jesus. (Ephesians 4:21)

So then, putting away falsehood, let all of us speak the truth to our neighbours, for we are members of one another. (Ephesians 4:25)

Above all, my beloved, do not swear, either by heaven or by earth or by any other oath, but let your "Yes" be yes and your "No" be no, so that you may not fall under condemnation. (James 5:12)

"The most important quality in a person connected withreligion," said Albert Schweitzer, "is absolute devotion to the truth. Being devoted to the truth is not an intellectual exercise; it is, as it should be, a living reality.

The "Judas" Way

An embrace! Think of being embraced in love's name. Then think of being embraced in betrayal: "The man I shall embrace is the one; take hold of him" (Matthew 26:48). And Jesus was arrested.

Judas chose an embrace to identify the master. An embrace—a sign of love, trust, and the joy of life—became a betrayal, a poison, and a death sentence. Why did Judas choose to betray Jesus with an embrace?

An embrace!

Judas loved Jesus—not totally—but he loved him. Judas had good times with Jesus. He had a very good position—a position many would have loved to occupy. He was in charge of the money. He was educated, cultured, skilled, polished, and belonged to a sophisticated society. He was not like the other disciples, who were fishermen, farmers, carpenters, uneducated people, ordinary people, people of the earth. Judas was the most articulate in logic and thinking. He liked to be considered above others, to be recognised in the crowd. He wanted to be special. He was special. This is the trouble. Someone who feels special, superior to everyone else, usually allows himself or herself to do whatever is not allowed for others. John, his colleague, says that "Judas held the purse, and used to help himself to what was deposed there" (John 12:6). When one is special, he can do that. His lie is not a lie; it is just a joke. His hypocrisy is not hypocrisy; it is loyalty to what is right. His secret greed for power and money is not a greed for power and money; it is a search for the common good. So it goes.

Judas tried many times to guide his master. He had better arguments than the master. When Mary at Bethany, for example, brought a jar of costly perfume and used it to anoint Jesus' feet, a strong protest came from Judas: "Why was not this perfume sold? It could have brought three hundred silver pieces, and the money have been given to the poor" (John 12:5). "What is the point of such extravagance? This could have been sold for a good price and the money given to the poor" (Matthew 26:8-9; see also Luke 7:37-38).

Who can argue with the necessity of helping the poor? Isn't this a very solid argument? Doesn't this sound familiar? A capitalist can use this argument. A socialist can use it. An independent can use it too. But Jesus had another view. He was not interested in the money, neither was he interested in perfumed oil. He was interested in the heart of that woman and her conversion. She was coming with a prayer, a song, and much love in her heart. And this is what really matters.

The head would not understand this. The head has its own reasons, different from the reasons of the heart. The heart's reasons are very subtle. One needs special eyes to see. Judas knew nothing about the heart. He was blind to the woman and her heart. He looked only at the perfume and saw how costly it was. This is what a thinker does. He calculates. Judas was a thinker, an economist, a political philosopher. He was convinced that he had a deeper understanding than Jesus.

Judas was certainly hurt. His ego was hurt. He gave the right advice to Jesus, and Jesus didn't listen to him.

He wanted the common good of the poor, and through this artificially good gesture, he wanted to satisfy his greed for power—his advice would have worked—and for money—he would have gotten his hands on more money. At the Last

Supper, he must have been very happy to have the master washing his feet. He was waiting for such a gesture, such a unique and "humbling" occasion from the master.

Judas loved money. But money was not really the only or most important reason for the conspiracy. He was too intellectual and too refined to be satisfied with just thirty pieces of silver. He must have had a more profound reason: when Jesus was gone, he would be in charge. Deep down, he was expecting to overthrow Jesus and take over his position. He wanted to be the head of the whole community. After all, wasn't he more educated and more cunning than Jesus? He needed to remove Jesus from the scene. He could not assassinate him, but he could sell him. Then he would have both the money and the power he really wanted. Why not? He was, after all, a "good" man. He was the most qualified, and he knew how to follow the logic of the mind and the code and rules of society's games. He was a politician, which Jesus was not. What can you expect from someone who says something like, "Love your enemies, pray for your persecutors" (Matthew 5:44). "Do to others what you would have them do to you" (Luke 6:31). "Be on guard against performing religious acts for people to see" (Matthew 6:1). "Do not lay up for yourselves earthly treasure" (Matthew 6:19). "Nothing is concealed that will not be revealed, and nothing hidden that will not become known" (Matthew 10:26). "What profit would a man show if he were to gain the whole world and destroy himself in the process?" (Matthew 16:26). "Whoever wants to rank first among you must serve the needs of all" (Matthew 20:27). "You shall love your neighbor as yourself" (Matthew 22:29). "Say, 'Yes' when you mean 'Yes' and 'No' when you mean 'No'" (Matthew 5:37), and so forth. This is not politics in this world of ours. Jesus was, for the world we have created, the worst "politician" ever to exist. Judas could be a successful leader and a good master in this world of ours. Jesus, the Master, is an unqualified leader and a poor master. He was a patent failure in this world of ours. He managed to end up dying on the cross.

Judas represents the ego. Judas knows how to compute, make compromises, lobby, and win. Jesus, here, is a loser. Judas can be a crafty businessperson, a foxy lawyer, a cunning and phony religious minister, or just an ordinary, greedy, opportunistic liar. Jesus can only be simple, direct, straightforward, and 'naive'—innocent. Judas exists in each of us. We are disciples of Jesus, as Judas was. We love Jesus, as Judas loved him. And we hate Jesus, at the same time, as Judas hated him. When you love someone, a part of you is going to be somewhat hurt because love requires a total surrender. When you move toward a total surrendering, somehow certain uneasiness arises. The ego resists. The ego starts to calculate. The power, the money, the prestige—the false self—are at stake. That part in us that becomes troubled by unconditional love is Judas. You start to think that "it is costly," "we could have used this for the common good." A Judas will give you the best speech on love. He will create a perfect how-to book on love. But he does not love because love is total trust. Trust is too risky for him. Judas loved Jesus, but not totally. He was divided. He lived a tragic dichotomy. To be able to betray, you must love first. No wonder he used the embrace as a signal. An embrace, a loving gesture, became a gesture of hate. The embrace translates very well the terrible dichotomy he was in, the split, the divided personality. As soon as Jesus was arrested and condemned, Judas committed suicide. Jesus, the object of his love and hate, was gone. And so was the meaning of his life. Emptiness leads to suicide, or, at least, to continuous unhappiness. This is what happens to some of those who are most articulate in logic and in thinking. The most learned people and the richest people, if they do not have love in their hearts, are also the most miserable people. Intellect, as important as it is, never satisfies a human being. The heart does. The mind can betray. Real love cannot betray. The mind agrees with Judas, the heart agrees with Jesus. The followers of Judas are in the millions because it does not cost much. Judas would say, "If you follow me, I'll give you this or that." The real followers of Jesus are just a few because they have to pay—with their lives, their very being. It is too risky! But when you pay it all, you have it all too.

Judas loved Jesus and hated him too. He embraced him. That ambiguous embrace was the beginning of Christ's crucifixion.

We, too, can be religious and we can accomplish all that is written in the holy books of religion, law, and tradition, and yet a Judas spirit may continue to live in us. It lives in all those who successfully play the religious game. It lives in those who religiously follow the rules, those who preach the rules, or those who enforce the rules. They do this not out of love for the rules, but for what they can gain from the rules.

The spirit of Judas lives in all those who pretend to love God before the eyes of the followers of God so that these followers become more generous in giving time and money. It lives in all those who become very rich with the money of the poor. It lives in all those who look so good on the outside but are ready to betray if more appealing interests arise. The spirit of Judas did not die when he died. We still betray.

We still give top priority to money. Every time we do that, we worship Mammon, not God.

No matter how we look at the story of Judas, we find something ironic in it. This man miscalculated big time; he did not get much for his money. He might have been happy for a few moments, then what? He went back to the temple and threw the money on the ground and confessed as loudly as possible that money did not offer him the happiness and security he was craving. Then what to live for? The curse of money!

In a sense, Judas may do us a favour if his story makes us re-examine our basic loyalty to our Creator. Do we sell our Creator for "30 pieces of silver" as Judas did? Do we betray God for a better job, a better position, a better anything? Do we betray God in order to foster our greed, selfishness, and self-centredness? Do we betray God for the "need" to be politically correct and compromise any principle and value we hold dear? What would it take for us to sell out God? What would it take for us to create our own god that is made in our own image? Does an incognito Judas live in us, here and now? Are we the close and familiar friends who know all the ins and outs of the Master and, because of this knowledge, have a better grasp of the method of betraying? Are we the ones who are blinded by the immediate results without seeing the consequences of our actions? Are we able to successfully live a double life and competently choose to walk the way of hypocrisy? What are our deeper motivations? What really drives our lives?

The "Pilate" Way

Pontius Pilate, the Roman governor of Judea who served under Emperor Tiberius from 26/27 to 36/37 AD, posed a question to Jesus before he handed him over to be crucified. The "What is truth?" (John 18:38), the question that Pilate asked during Jesus' trial, although simple in appearance, was a very profound question that was relevant at that time, remained relevant throughout the centuries, and is relevant today more than ever.

But what was the reason for asking this question, and how can one interpret it? When the Jewish religious leaders brought Jesus to Pilate, accusing him of blasphemy and asking the governor to execute him, Jesus asserted to Pilate, "Everyone who belongs to the truth listens to my voice" (John 18:37). Then came the crafty question, "What is truth?" (John 18:38). How can one interpret this question? Pilate could have asked this question out of genuine curiosity, seeking to know the very nature of truth. He could have asked the question out of personal struggle between right and wrong, when he was trying to deliver justice on a pragmatic level with the concern of maintaining social order. He could have asked the question as a cynical or mocking response to Jesus' audacious and straightforward statements about truth, in the sense of "Truth, eh? What's that?" He also could have asked the question because he was in doubt about the existence of absolute, objective truth, opting for subjective truths and moral relativism. In any case, Pilate could never have imagined the possibility that truth could be someone instead of something; it is a person, not a thing. What to do now, especially when he knew that this person in front of him was innocent and that he had received a message from his own wife to do this man no harm? Now the politician Pilate, who wants to appease people and keep his leadership job, got an idea: he would propose to the enraged people the choice between Jesus and the notorious criminal named Barabbas to be released, as was the custom at the Passover each year. If the people's choice was for Jesus to be released, Pilate would have diffused the situation very nicely. But the people's clear choice was Barabbas to be released, and not Jesus. The crowd went even a step further by uttering a subtle threat: "If you release [Jesus], you are no friend of the emperor" (John 19:12). Pilate got the message. "Then he handed him over to them to be crucified" (John 19:16). Pilate condemned a man he knew to be innocent. The Roman governor of Judea clearly was guilty of selling out an innocent man to save his own job.

The "Pilate" type knows the truth, thinks about it, and doesn't act according to it. Instead, this type would go hiding behind the "What is truth?" question, believing that the question would be an adequate exit for possible loss of the status quo, an eventual solution for a dilemma, or just a way to avoid responsibility. There is no doubt that Pilate's age-old question continues to be the big question of the day. Pilate was not the last person in history who, in order to pacify the crowd, delivered an innocent man to be crucified. A good majority of us, in order to keep the people happy, would practise the politically correct thing at the expense of justice and truth. Who hasn't met people who are convinced that there are times in life when compromising with the truth seems like a good idea? Who hasn't seen how often many institutions, in order to fit a culture, would go as far as to transmute a solid truth into a simple opinion? Who hasn't heard people say that one idea of reality is as good as another? Pontius Pilate will remain the champion of those who think that right and wrong are determined by circumstances, feelings, or personal preference, and especially those who do not match their actions with what they believe.

7| Liars' Ways (2)

Other dexterous and cunning ways liars love to use occur when they believe — and make you believe — that they are trying to be truthful to the common good and to the "truth."

The "Compromise" Way

We do compromise. When we don't, we usually let the "My way or the highway" approach run the show. Sometimes we even go much further than that.

When real dialogue is not possible, and when any hope for compromise vanishes, aggressive behaviours usually occur—including the possible annihilation of those who dare to oppose us.

Therefore, compromise is a great tool for making peace between people. It allows a convenient accommodation with others who co-exist under the same roof, in the same town, in the same group, in the same nation, and in the same world. It is normal to have different opinions since we have different backgrounds and ethnicities, different religions and traditions, and different cultures and ideologies. Therefore, it is normal that we don't think in the same way, we don't see the world in the same way, and we don't act in the same way. But we need to live in the same world. So, we compromise. From a human point of view, it cannot be otherwise, because no one can pretend to have the truth, the whole truth, and nothing but the truth. Consequently, compromise is good for us; our very survival may depend on it.

However, this is not the whole story.

It is a fact that a few of us compromise in the secondary matters of life, but not in the essential. It is also a fact that a good majority of us always feel ready to compromise in any circumstance and for any reason in secondary matters as well as in the essential. By doing so, we think we are pleasing everyone, and that then everyone will be happy and love us. But, as reality shows, this is not so.

The ancient Greek storyteller Aesop wrote a fable to prove that people who desire to make everyone happy will end up having no real friends after all. Please read with me this little fable entitled *The Birds, the Beasts and the Bat*:

> Many years ago, the birds and the beasts declared war against each other. No compromise was possible, and so they went at it tooth and claw.
>
> It was a terrible battle. Many a hare and many a mouse died. Chickens and geese fell by the score, and the victor always stopped for a feast.
>
> Now the bat had not openly joined either group as he did not want to be caught on the losing side. So when the birds asked which side he was on the bat quickly replied, "I have wings, I am on your side of course." And when the beasts asked who he supported, the bat responded, "with my sharp teeth and fur, it is obvious I am on the side of the beasts." The truth of it was that he did little to help either group spending most of his time telling tales about the other.

> When the battle was over, the conduct of the bat was discussed at the peace conference. The birds and beasts all turned angrily against the bat when they realized how many times the bat had changed sides and spread rumors. Since then the bat lives in fear of the beasts and the birds, hiding in dark towers and deserted ruins, flying out only in the night.

Living in the dark, as the fable suggests, is the downside of compromise. People of compromise do not like the light, so they hide in deserted corners. They prefer ambiguity, half-truths, and empty promises. They are everywhere on the map. Obscurity is their strategy, and a vague answer is their tactic. They are people of principles if necessary, and they are not people of principle if necessary also. They follow a particular ideology, and they don't. They are members of this or that religion, and they are not. They are with this or that policy, and they are not. They are very loyal, and they are not. They are your friends, and they are not. It all depends on the winds of the moment and the different circumstances.

But when are we allowed to compromise, and when are we not allowed? Why do we compromise in the first place?

Sometimes we compromise for material gain. Sometimes we compromise because of family ties and biased friendship loyalty. At other times we compromise out of fear, and at still other times we compromise because of our desire to avoid confrontation. Furthermore, we compromise because of a lack of faith, and that is the most dangerous of all. We may have a good heart and the noblest of intentions for saying and doing the right things, but if we compromise with the truth, "it won't work." Our mind does not create God. God exists whether we believe it or not.

God is a God of absolutes, and God is by far much bigger than all that we are able to understand and imagine.

But many of us prefer relativism. One of today's mantras would be: "You have your God and I have mine." That's for today—tomorrow is tomorrow. Here, most of us are very good "politicians." Politicians often change their position based on the political risks and interests. It all depends on the particular audience they are speaking to. Then, truth depends on circumstances.

This is precisely how compromise leads to deceit, legalism, ambiguity, procrastination, and dysfunction. Then a hypocritical, double lifestyle becomes accepted as the new normal and is justified as "not so bad after all" and "everybody does it and it is not the end of the world."

Compromise. Compromise. Compromise. We live in an age of compromise. Politicians compromise to secure votes. Police compromise to avoid riots. Employers compromise to prevent employees from unionising. Everyone is welcome. Every opinion is accepted. Every fashion is tolerated. Every lifestyle is authorised. Every behaviour is allowed. Every way of expressing oneself, or even worshipping, is permitted. The distinction between what is right and what is wrong is broken down, and there isn't a right or a wrong way to do things. Only the "politically correct" way counts. We do compromise, and we concede an inch here and an inch there, and a half-truth here and a half-truth there, following the path of least resistance. The spirit of the age seems to have taken over by pressing us to accept and live by the standards this world accepts and lives by. More and more, we tend to be like everyone else in this culture. We want to say what they say, think what they think, wear what they wear, act like they act, and live the way they live.

Somehow, we are becoming afraid to be different. Compromise. Compromise. Compromise. Nothing will pervert one's spiritual vision more than a spirit of compromise. It has the capacity to turn light into darkness and darkness into "light." The compromising teacher of truth will become—sooner rather than later—a disgrace and a detriment to the cause he or she has espoused. The very truth that is presented in a compromised way becomes a cause of rejection for the one who was supposed to embrace that truth. God Himself will be disregarded when God is conceived and presented in a compromised way.

Take another look at what the "old farmer" used to say: "God said it. I believe it. That settles it." Is this passé? If so, how would one explain?

> You must neither add anything to what I command you nor take away anything from it, but keep the commandments of the Lord your God with which I am charging you. (Deuteronomy 4:2)

> Every word of God proves true... Do not add to his words, or else he will rebuke you, and you will be found a liar. (Proverbs 30:5, 6)

> For truly I tell you, until heaven and earth pass away, not one letter, not one stroke of a letter, will pass from the law until it is accomplished. (Matthew 5:18)

> See to it that no one takes you captive through philosophy and empty deceit, according to human tradition, according to the elemental spirits of the universe, and not according to Christ. For in him the whole fullness of deity dwells bodily, and you have come to fullness in him, who is the head of every ruler and authority. (Colossians 2:8-10)

> Anyone who knows the right thing to do and fails to do it, commits a sin. (James 4:17)
> Adulterers! Do you not know that friendship with the world is enmity with God? Therefore, whoever wishes to be a friend of the world becomes an enemy of God. (James 4:4)

Modern science, theology, philosophy, psychology, and history contribute greatly to the understanding of a text. Who is going to doubt that? But any interpretation seems like a compromise when it tends to harmonise with the spirit of the world more than it does with the very word of God. In any case, science should not supersede Scripture, experience should not substitute for doctrine, and pragmatism should not dominate theology.

When it comes to the word of God, one cannot compromise. Accommodations and concessions are not the language that God uses, and they don't make anyone happy. The psalmist described the way by saying: "Happy are those whose way is blameless, who walk in the law of the Lord. Happy are those who keep his decrees, who seek him with their whole heart, who also do no wrong, but walk in his ways. You have commanded your precepts to be kept diligently" (Psalms 119:1-4).

No one is perfect, but making a mistake and failing to reach perfection is not the same as compromising convictions, attitudes, and lifestyles.

The compromiser who tries to live in two worlds gets shot at from both sides. It is not a good place where one wishes to be.

With the truth, there is no compromise—and there should not be. Jesus told us:

> Whoever is not with me is against me, and whoever does not gather with me scatters. (Matthew 12:30)
> For truly I tell you, until heaven and earth pass away, not one letter, not one stroke of a letter, will pass from the law until it is accomplished. (Matthew 5:18)

> If you love me, you will keep my commandments (John 14:15).

> You shall love the Lord your God with all your heart, and with all your soul, and with all your strength, and with all your mind, and your neighbour as yourself (Luke 10:27).

> If any want to become my followers, let them deny themselves and take up their cross and follow me (Mark 10:34).

> No one can serve two masters; for a slave will either hate the one and love the other, or be devoted to the one and

> despise the other. You cannot serve God and wealth (Matthew 6:24).

> Strive first for the kingdom of God and his righteousness, and all these things will be given to you as well (Matthew 6:33).

For Jesus, there is no compromise with the truth.

The "Complacency" Way

Beware of complacency; it is a killer. It will kill your relationship with family and others. It will kill your marriage. It will kill your relationship with God. As indifference, not hate, is the opposite of love, complacency, not death, is the opposite of life.

Toxic complacency!

Dictionary.com defines complacency as "a feeling of quiet pleasure or security, often while unaware of some potential danger, defect, or the like; self-satisfaction or smug satisfaction with an existing situation, condition, etc." Elsewhere, complacency was described as follows:

> Complacency is a blight that saps energy, dulls attitudes, and causes a drain on the brain. The first symptom is satisfaction with things as they are. The second is rejection of things as they might be. "Good enough" becomes today's watchword and tomorrow's standard. Complacency makes people fear the unknown, mistrust the untried, and abhor the new. Like water, complacent people follow the easiest course, downhill. They draw false strength from looking back. (Anonymous)

Complacency usually comes in two forms: self-satisfaction and self-defeat.

We have people who are at ease, self-satisfied, comfortable with things as they are, and they feel no need to improve the status quo. Because of their concentration on worldly pleasure and comfort, they seem blind—or they pretend to be blind—to the decay in society. In such a case, they will certainly be disturbed by any newness, freshness, renewal, and aliveness. A genuine and non-complacent religious person knows that God is calling him or her to something bigger than the current situation.

We also have people who feel self-defeated, overwhelmed by their difficult circumstances, depressed, tired of it all, and ready to give up. They tend to justify such an attitude by the "Why bother, since nothing is going to change anyway?" mentality.

Most of us may experience, from time to time, some kind of complacency. The real problem, however, arises when complacency becomes a way of life. Such a phenomenon was described this way:

> It [complacency] invades areas once occupied by our passion, interest, desire, and focus. When complacent, the valued things that had captivated our thoughts, hearts, and energies tend to fade from priority and can even become mundane or the boring routine of everyday life. Burnout in our work life, loss of fire in relationships, and the lack of zeal for things we once held important are common experiences. The shame is not in complacency

but in the failure to recognize it and take corrective measures to regain our footing. (Anonymous)

The Titanic is often remembered as an example of complacency. We built a ship with the most up-to-date technology available, and we declared the ship unsinkable. The ship carried lifeboats for 33% of the people who were on board. The "good enough" conviction and the special narcotic drug called "pride" led to the loss of 1,500 lives. The first symptom of complacency is satisfaction with the status quo and with things as they are. The second symptom is the rejection of any improvement and of things as they might be and must be. This means that each day is supposed to be a new day for growth and development. But instead, we choose stagnation. Beware of the hidden lie.

It takes energy and purposefulness to live a life without complacency. We lose that fire within, that once burned bright, when we are too busy, not busy enough, fatigued, bored, and especially when we take a partner or God for granted. Then, slowly and little by little, complacency sets in. We still do the work, duties and rituals, but love is gone. We run from someone (God, a spouse, a friend) to something (church activities, jobs, grades, investments). What was once first now becomes last. What was a priority no longer is. We then exhibit an attitude of self-sufficiency, which shows no real personal need for any relationship with God or with anybody. We think we can handle life and what it brings by ourselves, without the need of others or of God. We believe that constant dependence on others and on God is not part of reality; it is rather an imaginary need. When we don't think about God, everything ends up being about "me", my own comfort, my own well-being, and my own realistic or unrealistic desires. Beware of the hidden lie.

Complacency reveals that we are comfortable in the culture in which we live. When we align ourselves too closely with the philosophical systems and the lifestyles of the day, we lose the spiritual and critical evaluation of these things. We become content with the status quo instead of becoming vitalised and invigorated by the kingdom of God and its promises. When we are too settled in the lower, we stop striving for the higher.

Complacency is a sin against hope. It says there is no longer hope for a change. When we no longer have intimacy with God, when we are no longer part of God's purpose, and when we lose our motivation for making this world the kingdom of God, we, in fact, declare that we cannot change anything and that God is not involved in the world he created. This is a sin against God, because we think he is not doing anything, and against us, because we think that we are not able to change anything. We may still say "In God We Trust," but we no longer mean it. What a lie!

In spiritual life, there is no such thing as the status quo; either we go forward or we find ourselves going backward. If we get complacent, we may find that we have become lukewarm and further from God than we want to be. Here is the clear warning:

> I know your works; you are neither cold nor hot. I wish that you were either cold or hot. So, because you are lukewarm, and neither cold nor hot, I am about to spit you out of my mouth. For you say, 'I am rich, I have prospered, and I need nothing.' You do not realize that

> you are wretched, pitiable, poor, blind, and naked.... Be earnest, therefore, and repent. (Revelation 3:15–17, 19)

God invites us to know more (it is impossible to completely know the Ultimate), to be more (our world is in desperate need of saints), and to do more (choosing to put others' needs ahead of our own). God wants us to love, and we often choose to be pious over loving. Somehow, we find it simpler to be devoted than to be compassionate. We find it easier to read books on prayer or talk about prayer than to really pray. It could be more comfortable to find refuge in rituals and rules than to engage in the uncharted wisdom of love. No matter how hard we try to put God in the box of our theologies, philosophies, and the other sciences and disciplines, God is new every day and cannot be reduced to our so-limited understanding. God is love, and love has no limits. To think that we have arrived is a trap. Love requires an unceasing passion that rejects the lukewarmness of complacency.

There is often complacency within religious institutions. The fact that some institutions, while doing well with their programmes of social reforms and spiritual activities, for example, are unconcerned with the very word of God and personal holiness constitutes another example of complacency. We may think we are OK with God, but have we ever considered and pondered what God has to say about us? Complacency can be a subtle cause of apostasy from God throughout time, without being aware of it.

God wants to get to the roots of our dysfunction. God wants the total renovation of our lives, and he is not pleased by just performing philanthropic acts. Dustin Moskovitz says:

"There's a lot of complacency in philanthropy. People figure organizations are trying to do good, and that's enough, even if the results aren't there. But that's wasteful and inefficient. It crowds out better programs." Francis Spufford is even more direct when he says: "Christians are as subject to complacency as anybody else, and we can certainly settle into repetition and forget that something radical and extraordinary is being asked of us as well - that we hold to an extraordinary promise about how, from moment to moment, something enters the world and enters us, after which everything is different."

Being complacent with our situations and resigned to our fate is not what God wants for our lives. God wants us to align ourselves with the truth, do what is right, and be a blessing for others. God wants us to be living proof of his existence.

"The only thing necessary for the triumph of evil," said Edmund Burke, "is for good people to do nothing." These words can apply in every aspect of our lives. They apply in politics, in social justice and peace, in the struggle for freedom, in cultural and scientific pursuits, and in development and the environment. They also apply in our relationships with others and with God.

Evil triumphs when good people do nothing and remain silent. Such an attitude is not only complacency but also complicity; this is exactly what the enemy wants: to be happy with the status quo and remain silent.

Silence is good and recommended when centred, meditative, and focused on physical, mental, and spiritual health. But it is detrimental in the face of injustice, violence, sin, and all violations of the dignity and rights of humanity. Then it becomes an efficient contributor and accomplice in the expansion of evil. This is exactly what the enemy wants. Beware of the silent and sophisticated lie.

Complacency is not our ally but the enemy's ally.

Jesus was very harsh with the people of his time, more specifically the zealots, Pharisees, and Sadducees, precisely because they were not authentic people. Would he be more open-minded today and more compromising with the people of our age and culture? A resounding "no" would be the answer. Jesus always showed his strong opposition to disobedience to God and sin. He did not cave in to cultural pressure at that time, and he will not cave in to cultural pressure today. He was politically incorrect and irrelevant at that time, and he will be politically incorrect and irrelevant more than ever today. In the Kingdom of God that Jesus preached, God should always be first, and when God is first, everything else will fall into place.

When Pope Paul VI said, "Politics is the highest form of charity," he certainly wasn't talking about what is called "political politics" that places self-interest and personal ambitions before the common good and the service of others. A true politician should be a genuine person in the first place. He or she must have a higher consciousness to understand that love of neighbour should come before self-love, and that service of others is different from self-serving. He or she must have and display integrity and authenticity. In order to have such qualities, we should put God's will first, as Jesus did. For, as Charles Péguy put it, "Everything begins in mysticism and ends in politics."

The "Machiavelli" Way

What is more important in solving an issue: the end result or the process used?

This question has haunted human beings' minds for a long, long time and has never had one conclusive answer they could all agree on. Although the common assumption in Europe, for example, was that spiritual matters and eternal salvation were far more important than earthly success (power, money, pleasure), many answers have been offered throughout history with all their subtle casuistries and nuances. There was, however, one answer that seemed to stand out, carrying the life philosophy of Niccolò Machiavelli (1469–1527).

Machiavelli's most important book was *The Prince*. This book, written in 1513, was meant as a tract for the rulers of that time, but it has had a major influence on social and political philosophies all these years up to today. The author of this book seems to be a relevant inspiration for running our affairs in business, management, religion, education, and especially politics. Whether we admit it or not, many of us live the "Machiavellian way."

By lowering the standard of politics from the art of the good to the art of the possible, and from what people ought to do (the ideal) to what they actually do (the actual), Machiavelli became the guide-master of conduct for the people of his time as well as for ours. We too, in the footsteps of this political "guru," would like to assess the ideal by the actual rather than the actual by the ideal. Isn't this how our favourite philosophy of pragmatism was born, and what it is about?

In his mind and heart, Machiavelli thought that religion and morals were good for political life. But at the same time, in order to obtain good political results, he also thought it was important to break away from the traditional fixed morality of Aristotle and the Church. One of his main ideas was condensed in the famous phrase, "The end justifies the means." Even though Machiavelli may not have said it word for word, one can conclude after reading *The Prince* and some other works written by him that this is exactly what he meant to say. No wonder Machiavelli's name became, in the perception of many, synonymous with deception, duplicity, cunning tyrants, and those people who are ready to commit any possible atrocity in order to get what they want. Then, cruelty could be used in a creative way for the common good, the long-term security, and the greater prosperity of the state.

Moreover, Machiavelli seems like a source of inspiration and a favourite, if not "infallible," guide for those who seek to survive in the world as it is and not as it should be. He would suggest that anyone who ignores reality in order to live up to an ideal will, sooner or later, discover that he or she has been walking the path of self-destruction. This is why we talk now about the Machiavellian method that seems more relevant than ever in the way we live our lives. Machiavelli wouldn't be surprised to realize that we are becoming better now than in his time at justifying war or any other behaviour in the face of modern challenges. Also, we might be better at masking deep deceptions with declarations of virtue, integrity, and the common good. In this sense, it is probably fair to conclude that Machiavelli's legacy is the most "successful" hypocrisy of our time.

The reality is that, whenever a difficult situation arises, whenever an ethical challenge pops up, and whenever we have to make that critical either/or decision, the way we process this dilemma says a lot about us. It tells us about our values, our references, and our approach to life. It tells us where we stand in regard to others, and especially to God. It tells us our practical answer to fundamental questions such as: "Where do we come from?" "Why are we here?" "Where are we going?"

In such a context, we usually find ourselves in front of two basic ethical systems that are known as the deontological system and the teleological system.

The deontological system is grounded in the belief that the way we proceed and do things is more important than the result obtained. Therefore, no matter what the outcome might be, our actions must by themselves be good; goodness is inherent to the action no matter what the outcome is, and the conduct must be ethically good, not wrong, in the first place.

Some people think that the deontological system is absurd because it tends to consider the rules as ends in and of themselves, instead of being means to a greater end.

The teleological (also called consequentialist) system takes the opposite approach. Here, the consequences of our decisions and actions are more important than these very decisions and actions, which can be by themselves positive or negative. To decide whether something is good or bad, according to this system, we should look at the consequences of it, and not at some arbitrary rule or principle, and not even at some written script or constitution of the past. Therefore, if the result is good, even if we use bad actions, this system would consider our behaviour as ethical; and it would be unethical if the result is bad, even if we use good actions. In other words, it does not matter how we reach the end, as long as the desired result occurs, or, as it has been said, "It doesn't matter how you get what you want as long as you get it." In any case, the end will justify any means—good or bad, ethical or unethical, legal or illegal. What really counts, and the only thing that counts, is to be number one in all that we do at any cost, no matter what. "It is what is, not what ought to be, stupid!"

From a religious point of view, one can argue that the notion that good ends do justify any means, including evil ones, could be another definition of sin. Didn't Adam and Eve do just that? They sought the good end of knowledge by the evil means of disobeying God. Didn't Pilate do it also? He used, in spite of his conviction of the innocence of Jesus, the vote of the crowd—the Pilate's democratic method—to justify his surrendering to the crowd's demand to "release a prisoner" and to hand over an innocent "to be crucified" (see Matthew 27:15–26).

Isn't this what some of our leaders do in order to secure their leadership positions? They use a set of solid principles when such principles attract votes and support, and they use another set of pragmatic principles if the voters shift to different values. Isn't this what we also do when we sin? We do it because we want something good: "to be happy." Every sin—we usually consider it "a little sin"—is often committed with the aim of doing something good; we usually consider it "a big objective good." Things like power, money, comfort, sex, honour, security, getting information from terrorists, peace, are good in themselves, but not when we try to get them by disordered evil means.

Adolf Hitler thought he could resurrect his country, and have happiness, security, and peace for a powerful Germany by means of race war and mass murder. Joseph Stalin justified the killing of tens of millions of his own people by saying that the population was too large to be sustainable. Hiroshima and Nagasaki did end the war. Bombing German and Japanese cities reduced their munitions production. Abortionists are often happier and more prosperous. Judas did get his 30 pieces of silver. Jihadists think of paradise when killing innocent people or violating human rights. Saving, democratising, and modernising a country would be in the minds of those who want to get rid of an oppressive regime, no matter the cost, even if it was at the expense of very grave and heavy collateral damages. Alleviating suffering could be done, some people think, by the "compassionate" letting go of the elderly, the terminally ill, the miserable, and the unwanted. Feeding the hungry can also be done, for some other people, by robbing a bank and stealing goods from a supermarket.

Evil means can sometimes "work." Indeed, the reality is often in favour of the ones who use evil means; bad guys often win and come first, and nice guys often lose and finish last.

This is exactly the reality that the consequentialists count on and would like to use to prove their argument. They wish to go by a corrected version of what Jesus said. Their new version says: "What shall it profit a man to gain his own soul and lose the world?" In such a case, the persons who live the Machiavellian creed are those people who give themselves permission to bend the rules, deceive others, or use people for personal gain. They can use any means in order to achieve the strategic results. Therefore, by any means, "the end justifies the means."

Furthermore, we somehow have a tendency to convince ourselves that there is a clear dichotomy between the evil "them" and the good "us," as if "they" cannot do anything but evil and "we" cannot do anything but good. This dichotomy is nothing more than emotional judgement and does not correspond to reality. Still, our pragmatism (consequentialism) continues to be a favourite policy at the present time. We still argue that for the common good, these acts of torture, abortion, adultery, false witness, theft, violence, war, are permitted this one time and because of this special case—the perennial "special case."

Doesn't this sound familiar? No doubt, the ends/means dilemma is a very popular scenario in our lives in general, but especially in our political lives. Very often, we forget that, if a given end is justified, the means for carrying it out must be justified as well. If, for example, we have a principle like "do not violate someone else's property," we cannot override it by saying something like "but what I steal from this rich store can in fact benefit poor people who deserve it more." "We" are allowed to do it, but "they" are not.

Those who do not believe in God and His law may justify their actions by the good end they aim to achieve. However, those who claim to be children of God cannot break His commandments and His general order in the world. When God says, for example, "Do not kill, do not steal, do not commit adultery…" He did not add, "unless by doing so you will save a life, or you will advance a cause, or you will make peace." Objectively speaking, the age-old morality that consists of what God said it is remains, by far, a better path to follow in the long run than the fantasy of some pretender who thinks that this or that result proves much better in this or that particular circumstance. There are certain fundamental and objective principles that are "right" and "good," which are essential, and we cannot violate them. The Catechism of the Catholic Church states (#1753):

> A good intention (for example that of helping one's neighbour) does not make behaviour that is intrinsically disordered, such as lying and calumny, good or just. The end does not justify the means. Thus, the condemnation of an innocent person cannot be justified as a legitimate means of saving the nation. On the other hand, an added bad intention (such as vainglory) makes an act evil that, in and of itself, can be good (such as almsgiving).

In one of his very insightful articles, Professor Peter Kreeft rightly concluded that Machiavelli's way was the way of "morality [that] is based on immorality." He wrote:

> Social relativism also emerged from Machiavelli's philosophy. He recognized no laws above those of different societies, and since these laws and societies originated in force rather than morality, the consequence is that morality is based on immorality. The argument went like this: Morality can only come from society, since there is no God and no God-given universal natural moral law. But every society originated in some revolution or violence. Roman society, e.g., the origin of Roman law, itself originated with Romulus' murder of his brother Remus. All human history begins with Cain's murder of Abel. Therefore, the foundation of law is lawlessness. The foundation of morality is immorality. … No God, only man; no soul, only body; no spirit, only matter; no ought, only is.

How long can the world survive if it is ruled by the "… No God, only man; no soul, only body; no spirit, only matter; no ought, only is." How long?

There are no facts, only interpretations. Beware of the sophisticated lies.

Part 3: What Might Truth Be?

"I am the way, and the truth, and the life."

—John 14:6

8 | On Being Authentic

Authentic people are hungry for truth: truth in what they think, say, and do, and truth in their way of life. They know themselves. They know their strengths and they know their weaknesses. They have their goal, and they use their potential to achieve it. They live their ideal.

Authentic people keep their word. They live by "Let your word be 'Yes, Yes' or 'No, No'" (Matthew 5:37). Their word mirrors their minds and hearts.

Authentic people do not use the word "truth" as a weapon. They do not say phrases like, "I am just telling the truth," or "I am very honest, I just tell it the way it is." Under the guise of honesty, these statements can mean, "It's your fault, you blew it." People of truth do not use truth as a tool to hurt someone.

Authentic people start to be authentic with themselves first, then with another, and another, and another.

Authentic people live in the here and now. It is not that hard to live in the past or in the future. Nostalgia and reveries make us fail to experience life as it happens. This moment is really all that we have, and we ought to find and understand the relationship between being in the present moment and being our true selves. Guilt and preoccupation about the past, as well as anxiety and worry about the future, shift our focus away from the present.

But to live in the present moment does not mean to live solely by what our consciousness of the moment tells us to do, without any reference to God's will whatsoever. By being eager to harvest immediate gratification, we think that we are seeing the point of our actions. Often, that is not the point at all. It is not we who define what is right and what is wrong; it is God. Authentic people do not live by the "anything goes" philosophy. Their orthodoxy has solid references. It is also eschatological.

Authentic people are not afraid, not judgmental, and not critical of themselves and others. They appreciate themselves and others, have a great sense of gratitude for their blessings, and enough flexibility in managing their affairs and relationships.

Authentic people know that they are on a mission. They know their mission, and they do not feel completely fulfilled until this mission is achieved. Consequently, while comfortable circumstances may give them momentary happiness, their real delight is found in being genuine, true, and committed. Authentic people find their own voices. They have had their "Aha!" moment. For this moment of truth, they would say, they have come. That is why they make a difference.

Authentic people know what they want and how to get it through honest and open lines of communication, straight talk, and fostering meaningful relationships with the people in their lives. They believe in what they want more than they believe in what is.

Authentic people are not deceivers. Deceivers are people who mislead; they lead others to believe something that is not true. Deceivers are self-centred; instead of pointing to God as the centre of truth, they point to themselves as the way to truth. No wonder they end up distorting the truth. But, at the same time, they know how to cover up the distortion by half-truths and suitable lies.

Authentic people do not base their convictions or non-convictions on what others approve or do not approve. The Gospel of John illustrates this position well: "Nevertheless many, even of the authorities, believed in [Jesus]. But because of the Pharisees they did not confess it, for fear that they would be put out of the synagogue; for they loved human glory more than the glory that comes from God" (John 12:42–43).

Authentic people are people of conscience. They do not want to succeed at the expense of truth. In a document entitled *Conscience and Truth*, Joseph Cardinal Ratzinger (later Pope Benedict XVI) wrote: "A man of conscience is one who never acquires tolerance, well-being, success, public standing, and approval on the part of prevailing opinion, at the expense of truth."

Authentic people place tremendous emphasis on values. These values are the solid rock that holds them steady when circumstances change and the storms hit. Values give direction to their decisions, which are often different from what others would like. Values do not belong solely to ethics. They can be part of a correct appreciation of reality. Dietrich Bonhoeffer drew our attention to this question by saying, "'Telling the truth'… is not solely a matter of character; it is also a matter of correct appreciation of real situations and of serious reflection upon them."

Authentic people know that their experience of God grows and changes. This is why, while their beliefs remain very solid, they recognise the need and the importance of expressing the reality of God in different ways. Pope John

XXIII summarised this attitude beautifully in one concise phrase. He said, "The truths preserved in our sacred doctrine can retain the same substance under different forms of expression." Authentic people are adamantly attached to the truth, but they are not afraid to express it in a new way.

Authentic people do not fear discovering who they really are. Sometimes, we fear finding out who we really are, underneath all our masks and defences, and this causes us to resist being authentic and to live a hypocritical life.

The "cocktail" of our career, money, house, prestige, and the like that we identify with can be lost in seconds. But we still exist as we are. We should be able to say with St Francis, "I am what I am before the Lord. Nothing else, nothing more, nothing less." When we do that, we not only reduce the intensity of the fear of being the person we might discover ourselves to be, but we will accept being who we really are—no more, no less—and not someone else. Then, we will stop chasing after external life experiences that lead to lying and wearing masks that we think might make up for our inadequacies, and we will go straight to the heart of the matter: grasping the truth.

Genuineness and Self-righteousness

Genuineness is a quality of a right person. Self-righteousness is part of the "politically correct" lifestyle. A right person moves according to his inner world. He is in tune with himself. He is unified. He does not need to be a crowd. He does not pretend. He is true to himself and to others. He says yes when he means it and no when he means it. His behaviour translates what is going on within him. He is the worst politician imaginable.

A self-righteous person, when he is not right, is a very dangerous person. He is false, phoney, and hypocritical. He lives a double life: one for the world and one for himself. He possesses the art of hiding things. He tells you what you want to hear. His truth does not spring from principles. His truth corresponds to an external statistic and keeps an eye on the popular vote. He is a politician. He handles situations very well. He lives before the eyes of others. His reference is in his appearance and in the mask he wears. He is the most sophisticated, egotistical person in the world. He is moralistic. Deep down, he is able to condemn everybody. His morality is based on fear of punishment and hell, and maybe on greed, as his eye remains fixed on the rewards he can get from others and, later on, in heaven. His behaviour, instead of being an outcome of what he is, is the source of his action. He follows the rules. He who wants to play has to follow certain rules. A moralistic person plays the game of society. He follows the rules of the game. People believe he is religious because he often goes to the church and gives money to the poor. He knows how to gain respectability. He succeeds in wrapping himself in religiosity, even if his religion is only politics. His religion is part of his struggle to survive, part of his ambition, and a means of controlling others.

A self-righteous person is led by the law, although the law is not that bad after all. A right person is led by love.

Law is important to society and helps us to live in the world. But love is much more important to society and gives us, from outside the world, the reason to be in the world. Something from the invisible is needed. Law may come by logic, interest, and practicality. Love springs from mystery, the unknown, and the human heart.

By following the law, you are safe, respected, and righteous. By acting with love, your life will be poetry and dance. Law is your house. Love is your home. If you are lawful only, and nothing else, you will not be able to love anybody, because you lack spontaneity and magic.

You can prove the existence, necessity, and appropriateness of the law; it is usually a scientific matter. But how to prove love? Love is anti-science, anti-logic, and very often beyond law. A great scientist can love, can be full of love, but he can never prove it in his lab. Law makes you proud of yourself and your knowledge. Love makes you humble and reveals to you that you still do not know much about the real truth.

If you live by the law, you are going to be successful in the world. That is for sure. And if you live by love, misfortune is your fate. In the world, law succeeds, not love. People who live by calculations find that nobody can compete with them. They are successful in business, in politics, even in religion. People who live by love are sometimes failures. Law is social, dependable, secure. Love is wild, insecure, dangerous, and mad. Law makes you a good citizen and dictates to you how to behave with others. Love makes you a good person and tells you how to behave yourself in the first place. Law can be the foundation of society, but it can never be the spirit of it. Law is needed so that love becomes possible. The end is not the law, but love. Moses, who provided the law, was fulfilled by Jesus, who provided us with divine love, graces, and eternal truths. Law does not really prove God's existence. Only love does. God is love.

The norm of true morality is not, in the final analysis, fidelity to the law, but fidelity to the Spirit; that is, fidelity to the law of love that includes the other law, since "love is the fulfilment of the law" (Romans 13:10).

A right person reaches exactly this point. He is true to himself, to others, and to God, no matter what, even if he ends up on the cross, like Jesus. A righteous person prefers to be on the side of the secure law, no matter what, because he knows very well that this is the right way to be successful in the world, even if he is often the very cross.

Jesus was never more severe than with the righteous people, the Pharisees and Scribes. "The scribes and the Pharisees have succeeded Moses as teachers; therefore, do everything and observe everything they tell you. But do not follow their example. . .Woe to you scribes and Pharisees, you frauds!" (Matthew 23).

Only genuine people are accepted in the Kingdom of God, no matter how sinful their lives may have been. A deep morality of love is required. For the Kingdom, to be righteous is not enough. One is required to be right, genuine, authentic, and loving others with the very love of Jesus.

Authenticity Requires True Freedom

Only in true freedom can one flower. Freedom is probably the soul's deepest need. All of human history is the history of freedom. G.W.F. Hegel (1770–1831) put it this way: "The history of the world is none other than the progress of the consciousness of freedom." There are thousands and thousands of slaveries and people fighting for liberation. When you become free politically, the struggle does not cease. Only one type of slavery has been eliminated. But when you become free politically, you become more aware of other types of slaveries. And so, the struggle continues.

True freedom is not political, economic, social, psychological, or religious. It is not the licence to say whatever you want to say without censure. Even if all these are important aspects of freedom, they still do not equal true freedom. True freedom is a spiritual phenomenon. It has something to do with your innermost being. It is an existential truth. Political freedom is good in itself, as are wonderful economic freedoms, social freedoms, psychological freedoms, and religious freedoms. But none of these come close to spiritual freedom, which is freedom from things, objects, and oneself; freedom from being possessed by anything.

Detachment Is Freedom!

Any kind of freedom, except spiritual freedom, can be taken away. Is freedom that can be snatched away from you really freedom?

A spiritual freedom cannot be chained. It cannot be held in jail. True freedom remains true, even in chains and even in jail. Nobody can take your true freedom from you except you.

Do we really know what we are? We have been taught and trained to conform to the ways of others so thoroughly that we may not know what is our own way and what we want. Our parents, teachers, friends, books, TV, etc. are there to help us make the "right" decision. They even make the decision for us. And we pretend to be free. Freedom is freedom from one's false self in the first place. Freedom from the various social roles we usually identify ourselves with. Freedom from our programming, that collection of desires, motivations, expectations, ambitions, and demands on which our ego focuses most of our energy. Freedom from the "somebody" we strive to become. Freedom from the addictions and patterns we have unknowingly programmed as the path to our happiness. Freedom from the thoughts, ideas, opinions, and words that result from this programming. Freedom from our cherished notions, concepts, and assumptions. Freedom from our very self. Isn't this the meaning of one of Jesus' most penetrating sayings: "Whoever wishes to be my follower must deny his very self... Whoever would save his life will lose it, and whoever loses his life for my sake will save it" (Luke 9:23–24). In a sense, the less cultivated we are, the more real we become. The less idealistic we are, the more honest and authentic.

The most essential thing is not to make the self free, but to be free from the self. The seed, to grow, must lose itself as seed. Otherwise, no growth is possible.

When you reach your innermost centre, your ego loses ground. You are no more. The social factor that makes you what you think you are fades away. You would act from your heart, not from your personality. Your attitude becomes authentic, not a mere formality, a label, an etiquette. And when you say something, you mean it. Say 'Yes' when you mean 'Yes' and 'No' when you mean 'No' (see Matthew 5:37). You are free. It is a wonderful experience to live without a personality mask. You are freed from your own personality.

But this freedom has a price; freedom is never "free." Each moment of freedom is full of dangers. You may fall. But each moment is also full of possibilities. You may enjoy all kinds of growth. There are always risks. There is insecurity. There is the unknown. There is a possibility for error. But even to err, one has to be free, responsible, and conscious. That is why one fears freedom. Slavery is somehow comfortable. Somebody else takes responsibility. With freedom, one has to make his or her own choices. Then the struggle begins, and also the chance for peace. With the collapse of conditionings and all kinds of prejudices, there is a chance for peace indeed. Freedom, this kind of freedom, is the path to real peace. It is the opposite of prejudice.

True freedom is therefore a spiritual matter. You can be bound by circumstances and still be free. But if you are bound inside and free in circumstances, you are not free. You can have all the money of the world, you can leave your job and travel wherever and whenever you want, and have whatever you desire (as many people do), but this does not make you free. The outer circumstances help but do not affect you. Don't get yourself caught in others' opinions, not even in your own opinions, because opinions give substance to your belief. And if opinions crumble, you will be totally confused.

Stay alert. Remain free. Freedom is the real joy for human beings. It is the most challenging and appealing path to God. You can see God in freedom only when you start peeling away your self's masks until you reach the core of your being. God is right there. He is the essence of your being. Be free and "see."

No Real Freedom without Truth

Pilate's intricate question, "What is truth?" reflects the distressing perplexity of those who no longer know who they are, where they come from, and where they are going. We seem to have lost sight of the essential interaction between truth, the good, and freedom. We seem to have forgotten, as Pope John Paul II put it, that "Only the freedom which submits to the truth leads the human person to his true good. The good of the person is to be in the Truth and to do the Truth."

True freedom must be rooted in the truth about the human person, which cannot be rightly defined without the divine reference. The exhortation of Paul in this regard is clear: "Do not be conformed to this world, but be transformed by the renewing of your minds, so that you may discern what the will of God— what is is good and acceptable and perfect" (Romans 12:2).

The tragic aspects of human freedom are obvious. If the references to God, who is the truth, are disregarded, human beings will be driven by finite, limited, and ephemeral goods. Consequently, errors are unavoidable, and poor choices will run the show. Then, soon after, one will stop recognising God (see Genesis 3:5) as the source of truth, because freedom, the freedom that becomes absolute, will be the very source of human values. There is no bigger catastrophe than repeating the original sin in this way.

From this kind of freedom, which is slavery in its essence, Christ sets us free (see Galatians 5:1). But true freedom, in its true essence, is a reminder of and a development of the divine image in all of us who are created in this very image. Genuine freedom is in total and fundamental dependence on this truth. Jesus said it clearly and authoritatively: "You will know the truth, and the truth will set you free" (John 8:32).

Truth is so essential to freedom that without it there is no freedom. When he was still a Polish cardinal under the Soviet tyranny, Pope John Paul II said flatly: "There is no freedom without truth." Living free takes root in living in truth.

Truth is powerful not when talked about, but when lived. Truth is not an abstract virtue. If it were just an abstract ideal, we could be virtuous while asleep, as the Greeks pointed out. Truth means being a person of truth and becoming fully just, fully loving, and the best we can be in everything we think, speak, and do. In other words, we need to be fully human.

But how can we be fully human if we do not know the truth about what humanness is? Jesus, who was fully human and fully divine, mapped the way to that interconnection between human nature and divine grace. No wonder the Greek Fathers talked about our deification, or divinization, in Christ. St Athanasius (297–373) went so far as to say of Christ: "He was made man that we might be made god." This kind of anthropology stresses the fact that human persons realize their true existence in the measure in which they are raised up toward, and are united with, God.

Although this kind of perspective on truth sounds great and has the potential to offer a panacea for all diseases and malaises, and this is what it ultimately does—truth is, at least for many of us, a very painful experience. Before it makes us free, truth is capable of making us miserable first, and most likely it will. The reason for this is that truth exposes our hidden secrets, confronts our lies, and sees through our masks. This could be something ugly to face, and so painful that we prefer to run away from it and ignore it. Denial does not bring healing. Facing the truth does.

Only the person who is not afraid of the truth lives in it and is of its essence. This person is truly on a happy, healthy, and holy journey. A person like this creates an atmosphere of trust, where people are free to be truthful and truth can be told freely.

9 | "I Am… the Truth"

Once upon a time there was a very special teacher. This teacher chose a group of disciples and taught them the truth about God and about themselves, and how they were supposed to live their lives. He also drew crowds to himself and taught them how to love one another and how to care for the poor, the sick, the outcast, and everyone who was in need of help. Most of them did not understand. He taught them in parables; parables were easier to understand. Yet most of his listeners did not understand.

How can people understand when their own lives are crowded with twists and turns, uncertainties and distractions, and greed and self-centred interests? People fail to understand because of their own truths and convictions, customs and laws, and books and their own interpretations of the books.

This determined and resolute teacher persisted in his teaching until the day he revealed to them what the real truth was and who this truth was.

"I Am… the Truth"

To the question, "What is truth?" we usually hurry to answer something like this: we find truth in the reliability of information, or when we have no doubt about something, or when we have no reason not to trust, or when what was said corresponded exactly to reality, or when a special enlightenment occurred, etc. But to say that "I am… the truth" (John 14:6) is unheard of.

Could this be a bold claim of a man or what? No! Only God can say such a thing. Jesus Christ is the very embodiment of truth, and his life is the way to it.

Therefore, truth is not something, but someone, and we know that we are in the truth when we "have the mind of Christ" (1 Corinthians 2:16) and are able to say with Paul, "It is no longer I who live, but it is Christ who lives in me" (Galatians 2:20).

How can we have the mind of Christ and allow Christ to live in us? By following him, as he asked us to do (see Matthew 19:21), and imitating him in the path of love. He said, "This is my commandment, that you love one another as (italics mine) I have loved you" (John 15:12).

Notice the important use of the word "as" here. This word implies practicality and imitation, as in "If I, your Lord and Teacher, have washed your feet, you also ought to wash one another's feet. For I have given you an example, that you should do as (italics mine) I have done to you" (John 13:14-15). "As" also shows the degree of the love we should have for one another, which is supposed to be unconditional, and attests to the truthfulness of our discipleship. "I gave you a new commandment, that you love one another. Just as (italics mine) I have loved you, you also should love one another. By this everyone will know that you are my disciples, if you have love for one another" (John 13:34-35).

For us, disciples of Christ, the word "as" helps to define our true identity. We always need to turn to him in order to receive the answer to our questions about what is good and what is evil, what is true and what is false, and what is necessary and what is not.

The question, "Teacher, what good deed must I do to have eternal life?" (Matthew 19:16), asked by the rich man in the gospel, should be an essential question for us too. There is a deep connection between what we do and our destiny, indeed. The answer to this question also helps determine our identity existentially. It reveals the truth about ourselves. In his Encyclical Letter *Redemptor Hominis* of 1979, Pope John Paul II wrote:

> The man who wishes to understand himself thoroughly—and not just in accordance with immediate, partial, often superficial, and even illusory standards and measures of his being—must, with his unrest, uncertainty and even his weakness and sinfulness, with his life and death, draw near to Christ. He must, so to speak, enter him with all his own self; he must 'appropriate' and assimilate the whole of the reality of the Incarnation and Redemption in order to find himself. If this profound process takes place within him, he then bears fruit not only of adoration of God but also of deeper wonder at himself.

So, what is the truth about ourselves, about others, and about the world? The truth is not the reality perceived by me or you or her or him. No! The truth is the reality perceived by God. Only God can answer what is good, what is true, and what is beautiful, and that is because "No one is good but God alone" (Mark 10:18). Only God is able to see reality in all its complexity and dimensions. Our views are limited in space and time; this is why they are subjective and relative to circumstances. God's view is unlimited and eternal; this is why it is absolute and universal for all places and times:

"Heaven and earth will pass away, but my words will not pass away" (Matthew 24:35).

Here, we have a better understanding of Pilate's puzzling question, "What is truth?" (John 18:38), or, "What is that thing called truth? I have never heard of it before," he could have added.

Pilate's question can be seen as the reflection of our distressing confusion and perplexity when we do not know the truth about who we are, where we came from, and where we are going. Jesus mapped the road for us. He said: "For this I was born, and for this I came into the world, to testify to the truth. Everyone who belongs to the truth listens to my voice" (John 18:37). His voice is clear: "Sanctify them in the truth; your word is truth" (John 17:17).

Caught by an angry mob, Pilate missed the opportunity to listen to a man he described as "I find no case against him" (John 18:38).

Caught in the contradictions of our lives, we too very often miss the opportunity to listen to the word of God that is truth, exchanging "the truth about God for a lie and [worshiping] and [serving] the creature rather than the Creator" (Romans 1:25).

Worshiping and serving the creature rather than the Creator is an indication that we are not living at the centre, but from a whole conglomerate of many selves—the business self, the parental self, the religious self, the social self, the political self, and so on. Each self screams to protect its own interests. Consequently, truth cannot but be coloured by these self-interest realities. Only when we have the ability to make decisions out of the divine centre, and experience life at this centre, are we able to find the unifying reference point for all our many selves. Then, decisions emerge from a source deeper than our opinions, feelings, facts, and figures.

Christ at the centre allows our words and deeds to become one piece, because our life will then flow from the one single spring of truth. In his *Confessions,* Augustine wrote eloquently:

> And I looked at other things and saw that they owe their existence to you and are all bounded in you, not in a spatial sense, but because your being contains everything in the hand of your truth, and all things are true insofar as they exist, and the only meaning of falsehood is when something is thought to exist when it does not. And I saw that all things fitted in not only with their places but with their times, and that you, who alone are eternal, did not begin to work after the passage of innumerable spaces of time, since all spaces of time, both past and future, could neither go nor come without your permanent presence and operation.

Without an infinite reference point, no finite point has meaning; there is no solid basis for truth, morality, or even life. An atheist like Jean-Paul Sartre (1905–1980) can declare life meaningless, and Albert Camus (1913–1960), a fellow existentialist, was convinced that the real question in life was whether or not to commit suicide. Jesus gives meaning to life because he is the truth and the life (see John 14:6). He is not my truth or your truth. He is the truth.

In his life of 33 years on earth, Jesus was really angry twice; not when he suffered and was crucified, not when he saw the miseries of people—their sicknesses, depressions, frustrations, poverty, and sins. He was able to cope with the weaknesses of people because he understood the frailty and brokenness of our human condition. But there were two things he could not stand. With a whip of cords, he drove out of the temple all those who were making his Father's house a marketplace (see John 2:13–21), for "No one can serve two masters" (Matthew 6:24). Also, with very harsh words such as "Woe to you… you snakes… brood of vipers," he blasted the scribes and Pharisees, for they were "full of hypocrisy and lawlessness" (see Matthew 23:13–36).

Do we have the "Mind of Christ?"

We have, as human beings, the capacity to think, reason, discuss, choose, and act. What a gift this is! But there is a greater gift still—the gift of having the mind of Christ. This is the gift that is available to God's children, as St Paul affirmed, "But we have the mind of Christ" (1 Corinthians 2:16), and that makes all the difference in the world because then we will be able to think, reason, discuss, choose, and act as Christ did.

So, our mind—a combination of conscious and unconscious realities—directs our physical behaviour, because our actions are subject to our thoughts in the first place and take orders from them. What follows, then, is that if we want to imitate Christ or to be other "christs," we must think like Christ. We must have the mind of Christ.

What is the "Mind of Christ?"

There is a big difference between the way we think and the way God thinks. "For my thoughts are not your thoughts, nor are your ways my ways, says the Lord" (Isaiah 55:8). But how do we think like God thinks? "We must grow up in every way," says St Paul, "into him who is the head, into Christ, from whom the whole body, joined and knit together by every ligament with which it is equipped, as each part is working properly, promotes the body's growth in building itself up in love" (Ephesians 4:15–16).

To have the mind of Christ is to have the ability to discern the things of the Spirit of God as Jesus did. It is to think as Jesus did, to see things as Jesus saw them, and to conform our actions to God's will as Jesus did. It is to forgive as Christ forgave when he was on the cross. It is to give ourselves rather than to seek to receive, to serve others rather than to seek and compel others to serve us, to suffer for others rather than to cause suffering to others.

To have the mind of Christ means to have unconditional love for God with all our mind, heart, soul, and strength. It is to love our neighbour as ourselves and to do unto them as we want them to do unto us, and that includes our enemies as well. Moreover, all this should be done selflessly, humbly, and obediently. St Paul put it this way:

> Do nothing from selfish ambition or conceit, but in humility regard others as better than yourselves. Let each of you look not to your own interests, but to the interests of others. Let the same mind be in you that was in Christ Jesus, who, though he was in the form of God, did not regard equality with God as something to be exploited, but emptied himself, taking the form of a slave, being born in human likeness. And being found in human form, he humbled himself and became obedient to the point of death—even death on a cross. (Philippians 2:3–8)

To have the mind of Christ is to discern like him, to conceptualize like him, to talk to ourselves and to others as he talked to himself and to others, to hold beliefs about ourselves as he held beliefs about himself, and to command actions as he commanded actions.

When we have the mind of Christ, we are transformed by the renewing of our minds. As St Paul wrote, "Do not be conformed to the world, but be transformed by the renewing of your minds, so that you may discern what is the will of God — what is good and acceptable and perfect" (Romans 12:2). Then a radical change will take place within us and around us. We cannot remain the same, and our world will not remain the same. "The new self" emerges and we will realize how "Christ is all and in all." St Paul wrote:

> Do not lie to one another, seeing that you have stripped off the old self with its practices and have clothed yourselves with the new self, which is being renewed in knowledge according to the image of its creator. In that renewal there is no longer Greek and Jew, circumcised and uncircumcised, barbarian, Scythian, slave and free, but Christ is all and in all! (Colossians 3:9–11)

What Characteristics and benefits the "Mind of Christ" would have?

Having the mind of Christ, "In whom are hidden all the treasures of wisdom and knowledge" (Colossians 2:3), is characterized by many benefits that include:

- We will have "all the riches of assured understanding and have the knowledge of God's mystery, that is, Christ himself" (Colossians 2:2).

- We will have life and peace. The Letter to the Romans (8:6) tells us, "To set the mind on the flesh is death, but to set the mind on the Spirit is life and peace."
- We will be "complete in everything good," as St Paul wrote. "Now may the God of peace…make you complete in everything good so that you may do his will, working among us that which is pleasing in his sight, through Jesus Christ" (Hebrews 13:20–21).
- We will have the desire to live a life of obedience to God. "Turn my heart to your decrees, and not to selfish gain. Turn my eyes from looking at vanities; give me life in your ways" (Psalm 119:36–37). Not obeying God's laws means that we are following other laws. Following other laws means we have a different perception of reality that is dysfunctional and distorted because it is carnally minded. St Paul says, "The mind that is set on the flesh is hostile to God; it does not submit to God's law, indeed it cannot, and those who are in the flesh cannot please God" (Romans 8:8).
- We will be sure that we are in the truth. Jesus said, "I am the way, and the truth, and the life" (John 14:6).
- We will have abundant and everlasting life. Jesus said: "I came that they may have life, and have it abundantly" (John 10:10), and "Whoever believes in the Son has eternal life; whoever disobeys the Son will not see life, but must endure God's wrath" (John 3:36).
- We will allow the fresh living water to continue to flow in our hearts and souls. Jesus said: "Let anyone who is thirsty come to me, and let the one who believes in me drink. As the scripture has said, 'Out of

the believer's heart shall flow rivers of living water'" (John 7:38).

- We will be free. Jesus said: "If you continue in my word, you are truly my disciples; and you will know the truth, and the truth will make you free" (John 8:31–32).We will be happy. "My soul is consumed with longing for your ordinances at all times. Your decrees are my delight" (Psalm 119:20, 24).
- We will be able to say with St Paul, "For to me, living is Christ" (Philippians 1:21).

However, from another point of view, we should also be aware of some negative consequences of having the mind of Christ. Some of them are

- We will have opposition. The "worldly wisdom" will certainly oppose and persecute those who preach the truth of the gospel.
- We may expect great trials. To live godly in Christ is not a guarantee of living a good worldly life. St Paul's life, before his conversion, was much better, worldly speaking, than after he declared that he was for Christ.
- We will be the subject of all kinds of accusations, including even the accusation of having a bad spirit. This was one of the charges that was brought against Jesus himself.
- We will be subject to much misunderstanding. This is something to expect anyway. A selfish culture cannot, or does not want to, understand the principle upon which a true Christian behaves and acts. Who was more misunderstood than Jesus Christ?

- We will lose many friends. These "friends" would think we are extremist, intolerant, narrow-minded, too rigid, and the like. This should be expected also.

How to develop the "Mind of Christ"

Here are some ways to help develop the mind of Christ:

• On a daily basis, spend time with God in prayer, meditation, and reading and pondering the Scripture. Such a daily practice helps us to draw nearer and nearer to the divine mind by learning how God thinks and what is important to him. It is much more than just a kind of religious incantation. It is now a heartfelt communication with God that allows us to talk to him and hear back from him. Developing a personal relationship with God that leads to incredible intimacy with him is the best way to develop the mind of Christ in us.

- Read and ponder writings of great spiritual men and women. These writings are usually scripture-saturated and Christ-exalting. They point the way to develop the mind of Christ in us by providing practical suggestions and methods on how to imitate him.
- Spend time with God's people and talk about the things of God. Ask questions and hear answers. Listen to what they say not only from a theoretical point of view, but especially from an experiential point of view. You will learn from them how to develop yourself in the things of God.
- Have a strong desire for knowing God, a desire that leads to the Christian discipline that fosters the intimate relationship with God. "When you search for me, you will find me; if you seek me with all your heart, I will let you find me, says the Lord" (Jeremiah

29:13-14). If we have the determination, God will help us achieve the objective of our sincere desire by doing in us and for us what we cannot do for ourselves.

- Recognize that the mind of Christ is a state of mind that needs to be protected. The book of Proverbs (4:23) reminds us, "Keep your heart with all vigilance, for from it flow the springs of life." Our numerous distractions have the potential to prevent us from having the mind of Christ. Indeed, by consuming large volumes of precious moments of our lives and by keeping us from thinking for ourselves and appreciating in-depth spiritual enrichment, our televisions, radios, and computers, to list only a few, constitute a real distraction from having the mind of Christ. We are supposed to be in control of these media and not allow them to control us. In the same way, we should be in control of choosing the people we want to be with. These too can be a big distraction from having the mind of Christ. All in all, we must decide that we are the holy place where God can dwell without counterfeit gods, false idols, and sources of distraction.
- Submit your mind to frequent tune-ups. Examinations of conscience and confessions are like performing a computer virus scan, which detects malicious "infections" throughout the system. When the virus (sin and other irregularities) is found, we should take the appropriate action to disinfect and repair the damage. Retreats, meditations, conversations with a spiritual director, and of course prayers are the anti-virus programs we can count on for regular

maintenance. They also help us to empty the trash folders and focus again and again on the "only one thing" that is needed (see Luke 10:42).

All in all, we should say that the problem with our mind is not merely that it is finite and incapable of seeing at once all the information and data. The problem and solution is that our mind has what we call a "mindset." This does not mean only that it has a certain viewpoint, but also a certain posture, an attitude, and a bent, a "spirit." This is where St. Paul wanted to go when he called attention in Ephesians 4:23 to "be renewed in the spirit of your minds." So, our very mindset, bent, attitude, the spirit of our mind, should always be God's perspective, not our perspective.

Living the Truth

Since God is truth, God's people are called to live this truth, which is God's word. "Sanctify them in the truth; your word is truth" (John 17:17). "I trust in your word. Do not take the word of truth utterly out of my mouth, for my hope is in your ordinances" (Psalms 119:42-43). "O send out your light and your truth; let them lead me; let them bring me to your holy hill and to your dwelling" (Psalms 43:3).

The disciples of Christ, created in the image of God who is The Truth, live in the "Spirit of truth" who leads "into all the truth" (John 16:13). Truthfulness and sincerity, then, which lead to showing ourselves true in words and deeds, oppose all duplicity, dissimulation, and hypocrisy, and keep "a clear conscience toward God and all people" (Acts 24:16).

Also, having put on "the new self, created according to the likeness of God in true righteousness and holiness"

(Ephesians 4:24), the disciples of Christ "[put] away falsehood" (Ephesians 4:25) and "rid [themselves] of all malice, and all guile, insincerity, envy, and all slander" (1 Peter 2:1). So, they will avoid any rash judgment, detraction, calumny, and perjury, and they will respect others' reputations. They do this by forging honest selves, the way God created them to be. When one is in the image of God, falsehood is supposed to quickly vanish, because no darkness can resist a single flash of truth.

The disciples of Christ admit they are sinners. They take responsibility for their wrongdoings. They are clear about what they are; they do not define themselves by what others say about them. They know that a need for approval may keep them from speaking the truth and acting on their convictions. Their identity is not based on the applause of others, nor is it diminished by lack of recognition or even insults. They are completely unconcerned, perhaps even indifferent, about polls and statistics. They care greatly about the truth in others by loving them greatly. So, truth frees them from such a need and allows them to feel a deep sense of security.

Paul was secure about his identity in Christ when he wrote: "By the grace of God I am what I am, and his grace toward me has not been in vain" (1 Corinthians 15:10). He knew who he was. He was not afraid to say it. His true self radiated honesty and integrity, which became a way of being, a way of looking at the world, and a way of growing in truth and authenticity.

With a healthy self, one sees the present as it is but works to transform it to what it ought to be. He or she does it with love. Truth may hurt temporarily, but it remains in the long run the best policy and certainly the best healing agent for individuals and for communities and society.

Integrity calls people to know who they truly are, be at home with their true selves, and shape the world in their image, which is a reflection of the image of God. By closely following Christ, one does not go astray, as mystic and theologian Richard of St. Victor (d. 1173) suggested: "If you are in a hurry to reach higher things, you will go safely if truth goes ahead of you. Without truth your labour is in vain. Truth does not want to deceive, and so it cannot be deceived. If you do not want to go astray, follow Christ." When we follow Christ, we start to see as God sees. Here, Meister Eckhart (1260–1328), one of history's great mystics, cannot help but say unambiguously:

It is your destiny to see as God sees,
to know as God knows,
to feel as God
feels.
How is this possible? How?
Because divine love cannot defy its very self....
Every object, every creature, every man, woman and child
has a soul and it is the destiny of all,
to see as God sees, to know as God knows,
to feel as God feels, to Be
as God
Is.

So, the real guarantee of truth consists in not taking our eyes off Jesus.

Also, the disciples of Christ are witnesses of the gospel. They are contemplative in action. The words in the holy book do not remain words on a page. They become a living reality that makes truth known, seen, touched, experienced, lived for, and died for. What witness to the truth is stronger than martyrdom! St. Ignatius of Antioch said: "Let me become the food of the beasts, through whom it will be given me to reach God."

In essence, truth is a living argument rather than a theoretical one. In this sense, G. K. Chesterton was right when he observed: "The best argument against Christianity is Christians," and he added: "The best argument for Christianity is Christians." This means that we should speak and live God's truth in all areas of our lives. To live any other way is to live a lie.

To live the truth seems impossible for humans, but not for God. God's grace is there for the asking. God's grace transforms. It did for Paul: "For I am the least of the apostles, unfit to be called an apostle, because I persecuted the church of God. But by the grace of God I am what I am, and his grace toward me has not been in vain. On the contrary, I worked harder than any of them, though it was not I, but the grace of God that is with me" (1 Corinthians 15:9–10).

The monumental question, "What is truth?" that was asked by Pontius Pilate, the Roman governor of Judea, before Christ's crucifixion continues to haunt people's minds throughout the centuries in pursuit of the ultimate meaning of life. The Holy Bible reveals that "truth" is a Person, a message, and a way of life. Jesus said it, "I am the way, and the truth, and the life" (John 14:6).

10| Transformed by Truth

One true thing about truth is that it can very often be unpleasant, unpleasant for its messenger and especially unpleasant for its receiver. Imagine the embarrassment and shame of King David when Prophet Nathan, pointing an unhesitant accusing finger at him while David was trying to hide his sin, said, "You are the man" (2 Samuel 12:7).

Prophets are the enemies of others' whims and illusions, just as surgeons are the enemies of their patients' abnormalities and diseases. Their knife of truth is the first step to healing. When Jesus said that he was bringing a sword (see Matthew 10:34) to this earth, he was talking about that knife of truth, which has the power to tear off masks, shred illusions, and cut off the root causes of our malaise and unhappiness.

The illusions of righteousness blind our view. In order to help us see, it takes Christ's sharp blade to perform a critical surgical operation and remove the veil that shrouds our minds (see 2 Corinthians 3:15–16).

The use of that sharp blade cannot be more unpleasant. Indeed, the removal of the very "morality" and "religiosity" that have successfully served our selfishness may cost us much bloody emotion. But we know that this is how we are going to heal. Christ's knife of truth will heal the wounds it inflicts.

Do We Really Know the Truth about Ourselves?

The well-known phrase "Know thyself" expresses the essence of Socrates' philosophy, whose real mission was to know the truth about human existence and transform men and women into moral beings. This is why he also said, "An unexamined life is not worth living."

Once we truly know ourselves, we may be able to care for ourselves. Otherwise, chances are we won't.

Self-knowledge is not an end in itself, but a road that leads to transforming a person's existence by practising virtues such as moderation, courage, justice, intellectual consistency, compassion, and truthfulness. How can a person reach his or her full potential and live a fulfilled life if this person does not know who he or she is and what his or her purposes are?

There is a deep connection between this kind of knowing and doing. Knowing modifies doing. There is much more at risk in knowing oneself and what is right or better and what is wrong or worse for oneself, than in, let us say, buying things or changing a career. One's whole destiny is at stake; that is the difference.

When one knows the answer to the age-old question, "Who am I?" one will start to see the truth about what really matters, about whether or not one is living the life his or her heart is longing for, and about whether or not one should find better paths to improve his or her way of being.

Failing to know oneself in depth leads to telling lies to oneself and to others.

Living a life of lies is the source of many of our greatest problems and diseases. Intimacy vanishes. Connections break up. Motivations are lost. Tension, burnout, and fatigue encroach. Respect at work disappears. Authenticity, self-esteem, and the sense of self-worth fade. Depression and its consequences creep in.

Healthy people are honest with themselves. They tell the truth about themselves, to themselves, first. Truth does not scare them; it frees them. They search for what is real in their responses to life. They are not fulfilled otherwise.

At the age of 19, Tatiana, who was born Tajci in Croatia, became a superstar in Central Europe. Her concerts, video shoots, and personal appearances were enormously successful. She attracted huge numbers of adoring fans, especially among young people who were looking to her for answers. But she had no answers for them. The "dream come true" she enjoyed did not fill the hole of emptiness and loneliness she felt in her heart. Her celebrity status was not giving her the satisfaction she wanted. She was not living her truth.

One day, at age 21, she decided to leave behind fame and glamour and all they offered. She came to the United States alone, under a different name, and completely unknown. Anonymity, prayer, and faith brought her the freedom to find the truth about what God wanted her to be. The realization of her true self inspired her to compose music, sing about her new experiences, and share her faith in concerts in hundreds of churches.

Without a clear look at her internal truth and true self, Tatiana's other selves and unconscious desires would have continued to run the show. There is no real freedom, internal or external, without truth.

The trip into the "holy of holies" of ourselves may be painful, or an action that we often are afraid to take, but it is critical in helping to make us healthy, happy, and holy. Truth will turn a person into a truthful one.

In the "holy of holies" of our being, "We are not who we know ourselves to be," wrote Henri J. M. Nouwen beautifully, "but who we are known to be by God." Explaining more, he said:

> We are not what we can acquire and conquer, but what we have received. We are not the money we earn, the friends we make, or the results we achieve; rather, we are who God made us in God's infinite love. As long as we keep running around anxiously trying to affirm ourselves or be affirmed by others, we remain blind to the One who has loved us first, dwells in our heart, and is indeed our true self.

Some of the masks we put on are known to us, but the majority of them are unconscious creations. There is no better place to learn how to take them all off, and get rid of them, than in the home-ness and safety of the body of Christ. It is crucial to understand ourselves from God's point of view, not ours. Here are some of the lies we, knowingly or unknowingly, say about ourselves and the truth that God wants us to live by:

UNTRUTH	TRUTH
I am worthless.	"Then God said, 'Let us make humankind in our image, according to our likeness'" (Genesis 1:26).
I feel defeated and paralyzed.	"For God did not give us a spirit of cowardice, but rather a spirit of power and of love and of self-discipline" (2 Timothy 1:7). "But thanks be to God, who gives us the victory through our Lord Jesus Christ" (1 Corinthians 15:57).
I'll always fail and I'll never change.	"I can do all things through him who strengthens me" (Philippians 4:13). "The Lord will fulfill his purpose for me" (Psalms 138:8).
Walking in the truth does not seem to give me results.	"The one who is righteous will live by faith" (Galatians 3:11).
God is not going to keep forgiving me.	"If we confess our sins, he who is faithful and just will forgive us our sins and cleanse us from all unrighteousness" (1 John 1:9).
I feel overwhelmed, and like I am losing my mind.	"Those of steadfast mind you keep in peace — in peace because they trust in you" (Isaiah 26:3).
I don't feel I am standing on solid ground.	"Trust in the Lord forever, for in the Lord God you have an everlasting rock" (Isaiah 26:4).
I quit. Who cares? Does God care?	"Be steadfast, immovable, always excelling in the work of the Lord, because you know that in the Lord your labour is not in vain" (1 Corinthians 15:58).
God won't use	"My grace is sufficient for you, for

me if I'm not strong.	power is made perfect in weakness. So, I will boast all the more gladly of my weaknesses, so that the power of Christ may dwell in me" (2 Corinthians 12:9).
To be accepted, I have to be perfect.	"If we say that we have no sin, we deceive ourselves, and the truth is not in us" (1 John 1:8).
I constantly look for others' approval.	"Am I now seeking human approval, or God's approval? Or am I trying to please people? If I were still pleasing people, I would not be a servant of Christ" (Galatians 1:10).
Everybody's doing it.	"You shall not follow a majority in wrong doing" (Exodus 23:2).
What is the point in telling the truth when everybody lies?	"I do my best always to have a clear conscience toward God and all people" (Acts 24:16).
No one loves me.	"I have loved you with an everlasting love" (Jeremiah 31:3).

God's word is not something we passively listen to or read on a page of a book. God's word is powerful. It forms and shapes our understanding as Christians. It defines our identity as human beings from God's point of view. It generates life, produces change, cleanses minds, heals hurts, builds character, nourishes souls, and brings fulfilment. James pointed out, "In fulfillment of his own purpose he (the Father of lights) gave us birth by the word of truth, so that we become a kind of first fruits of his creatures" (James 1:18). One can die not only from hunger, but also from junk food. This is why one should count on no other but the word of God for true nourishment.

The Scripture was not given to us to increase our knowledge of God, although this is what it does too. The Scripture was given to us to radically transform our lives (see 2 Corinthians 3:18) by making us loving people. Love defines us as it defines God.

In the body of Christ, the greatest commandment is to love God with all our hearts and minds, and to love others as ourselves. Love makes others feel safe. The safer they feel, the less their need for masks as mechanisms for self-protection.

When we know the truth about ourselves as children of God, and we know the truth of God's love for us, which is a fundamental truth of our identity, and that love is to reach others, we show them that we are Christ to them as they are Christ to us. Now that's even beyond simple transparency. "Now the Lord is the Spirit, and where the Spirit of the Lord is, there is freedom" (2 Corinthians 3:17). What a realization!

The real miracle that transforms our lives is when we turn to God to ask the question of the secret of our being, and we hear the answer in quiet intimacy: "You are my beloved children."

Being a "beloved child of God" is the miraculous truth that is at the base of every imaginable fulfilment and cure of any malaise.

Our general well-being and health are dependent upon seeing the truth that we are the beloved children of God. Jesus told us, "The eye is the lamp of the body. So, if your eye is healthy, your whole body will be full of light; but if your eye is unhealthy, your whole body will be full of darkness" (Matthew 6:22-23). Do we have healthy eyes to see our truth in God? Don't we know that we are not what others say we are, but what God says we are?

Finding our identity in God is, therefore, critical for our general well-being. This truth frees us from the need for others' approval to define us, from the urgency of any kind of possessions or power to describe our essence, and from the obligation to meet the expectations of our society to live our true purpose in life. The truth is that we are citizens of the kingdom of God and we live by the golden rule of the kingdom, which is love.

In the kingdom of God, logical principles and ideologies do not work if they are not in concert with love, because reality itself is grounded in God, and God is love, not an abstract concept or a logical system. That is why living by just principles does not always lead to truth. Love always does. Love is the basis for the ability to perceive the truth in its essence in all aspects of life.

God is "the way, and the truth, and the life" (John 14:6) and "God is love" (1 John 4:16). Any other understanding of God is a deformed mental exercise and a bad, hypocritical practice. One can make a very good living with a "politically correct" lifestyle, but one cannot make a life.

The Secret of Our True Being Revealed

Do I really know who I am? Do my actions say something about me? Do my actions and reactions run my life? Am I aware of my deep feelings and motivations? Does my outer self reflect my inner self? Do I realize that the way I see things and live my life does not just happen, for it is a result of what and who I am?

Such questions are very challenging for all of us.

To find myself, to know myself, and to be myself is the greatest discovery, indeed. After all, I may not be really me or what I seem to be. I inherited most of what I call "me." Clearly, my ideas have belonged to someone else. My behaviour is conditioned by my community. If I had been born in a different place, a different time, and under different circumstances, I would have had different tastes and criteria for liking and disliking. My concepts and ways of thinking have preceded my birth. My reactions and lifestyle have been a direct result of my training. My house, my car, even my clothes and all that I call mine are not made by me. I did not choose my parents. I did not choose the place and times of my birth. So, how can I pretend to know the whole truth about myself and define who and what I really am?

Psychologists and counsellors can certainly aid in helping me to better know myself. But the most satisfying way to get to the truth of myself is to ask the one who himself, about 2000 years ago, asked the question, "Who do you say that I am?" (Matthew 16:15), to those who were the closest to him and who knew him best.

"Lord, who do you say that I am?" You know everything about me. You know my past, my present, and my future. You know my realities and my dreams. You know my fears, failures, and struggles. You know my desires, my whims, and my hopes. You know my sins and blessings. I want to be who I am supposed to be. How can I be that person if you do not tell me who I am? No psychologists and no science can be completely trusted to answer me. There is no real cure for my problems if I do not know the whole truth about myself. I want to know myself. I want to be myself.

A prayerful relationship with God is the way to know ourselves best, and to be awakened to the whole truth about our very existence, destiny, and healing. Jesus asked the people he met to leave behind what kept them from themselves and open their hearts and minds to claiming their status of being beloved children of God.

When werealize, beyond the shadow of a doubt, that we are these beloved children of God, and that God loves us unconditionally and cares for us completely, we dare to let ourselves be carried by the winds of grace, the source of all healing and transformation.

We know, then, that we are to live the present moment in all its fullness. We are free from the conditionings of yesterdays and the worries of tomorrows. We dare to say, "Give us today our daily bread," and we mean it, for "[our] heavenly Father" takes care of his children as he takes care of the "lilies of the field" and the "birds of the air" (see Matthew 6:25-34).

The real miracle that transforms our lives is when we turn to God to ask the question of the secret of our being. We hear the answer in quiet intimacy: "You are my beloved children."

Being a "beloved child of God" is the miracle truth that is at the base of every imaginable fulfilment and cure of any malaise.

Our general well-being and health are dependent upon seeing the truth that we are the beloved children of God. Jesus told us, "The eye is the lamp of the body. So, if your eye is healthy, your whole body will be full of light; but if your eye is unhealthy, your whole body will be full of darkness" (Matthew 6:22-23). Do we have healthy eyes to see our truth in God?

Finding our identity in God is, therefore, critical for our general well-being. This truth frees us from the need of others' approval to define us, from the urgency of any kind of possessions or power to describe our essence, and from the obligation to meet the expectations of our society to live our true purpose in life. The truth is that we are citizens of the kingdom of God and we live by the golden rule of the kingdom, which is love.

In the kingdom of God, logical principles and ideologies do not work if they are not in concert with love, because reality itself is grounded in God, and God is love, not an abstract concept or a logical system. That is why living by just principles does not always lead to truth. Love always does. Love is the basis for the ability of perceiving the truth in its essence in all aspects of life.

"I Am Making All Things New"

The Incarnation began with Jesus, the newborn baby of Bethlehem, and has continued for more than twenty centuries. God is still here among us because he said, "And remember, I am with you always to the end of the age" (Matthew 28:20), because the Eucharist is always here, and because we are "the body of Christ's and individually members of it" (1 Corinthians 12:27) with the assignment to keep him in the world as Jesus did.

God still has human skin and still walks the earth among us, touches us, listens to us, hugs us, looks deeply through our eyes into our brain, heart, and soul, and heals us, as Jesus did; "Truly I tell you, just as you did it to one of the least of these who are members of my family, you did it to me" (Matthew 25:40).

God was visible in Jesus and is still visible in the Eucharist and in the other who is Christ in disguise, as St. Mother Teresa of Calcutta would like to say. God once acted through Jesus and he now acts through those who imitate Jesus, think like Jesus, and act like Jesus. And, as Ronald Rolheiser insightfully wrote:

> The God of the incarnation has real flesh on earth and speaks to us in the bread and butter of our lives, through things that have skin—historical circumstance, our families, our neighbors, our churches, and that borderline-psychotic friend who painfully reminds us that we are not God.

It is true that, very often, we go seeking God in monasteries, retreat centers, books, theories, systems, the far sky, and in the extraordinary—of course he is there since he is everywhere. But he is also much closer to home. He is incarnate in the ordinary events of our daily life. He lives in the here and now of a family, a community, a nation—this very world. God is not only in heaven. God is also on earth. St. John describes this incarnate God by using very revealing words. He wrote: "Those who say, 'I love God,' and hate their brothers or sisters, are liars; for those who do not love a brother or sister whom they have seen, cannot love God whom they have not seen" (1 John 4:20). This means, in substance, that God has a human face: loving God requires loving others. But to be able to do that, one must "incarnate" God in himself or herself first. Then it wouldn't be enough to read, or to hear someone telling us about, what God wants. Now we want our eyes to be God's eyes so that we can look at things the way God looks at them. No wonder we would discover something that was invisible to us and to others, and we would realize that everything is sacred because "The earth is the Lord's and all that is in it, the world, and those who live in it" (Psalm 24:1).

We do not understand the mystery of the Incarnation if we do not see the immensity of its implications. Divinity in human nature means the full potentiality and openness of our nature to the possibility of what the Greek Fathers termed "deification" or "divinization." "[God] was made man that we might be made god," dared to say St. Athanasius.

So, a birth of new consciousness—"the mind of Christ" (1 Corinthians 2:16)—is needed. This will uplift the entire world.

Imagine a world without ugly wars, terrorism, and violence of any sort. Imagine a society without poisoned racism, dishonesty, adultery, and gender confusion. Imagine a leadership without malignant political correctness, intellectual intimidation, and self-serving interest. Imagine a community without insane "religion," a double-faced way of living, and self-destructive lifestyles and behaviors. Imagine a nation without a leadership deficit, a budget deficit, and character deficit. Imagine a world without the counterfeit gods of money, power, prestige, pleasure, and the never-ending greed forever "more." Imagine a world without lies—intentional or unintentional—without robberies—seen or unseen—and without hypocrisy—palpable or hidden. Imagine a world "where righteousness is at home" (2 Peter 3:13), where Yes is Yes and No is No (see Matthew 5:37), and where truth is known—a truth that makes us free (see John 8:32). Such a world is not a world that has undertaken a sheepish reform of a sort, or even some kind of cosmetic surgery. This is a new world altogether; for "a new creation is everything" (Galatians 6:15). "I am making all things new" (Revelation 21:5). Wouldn't it be the world that we were waiting for, as St. Peter says, "In accordance with his promise, we wait for new heavens and a new earth" (2 Peter 2:13)?

In a world that operates according to the "mind of Christ"—the philosophy of Jesus—people would have clear references for discerning right from wrong. So, in vain we would go on searching for the truth in ideologies, political systems, or even "religions." It is not there. And it is not in what "you" think it is either, nor is it in what "I" think, nor in what "we" think, nor in what "they" think. It is not there. The truth is found in the word of God who said, "I am the Lord your God.... You shall have no other gods before me" (Exodus 20:2,3), and in the Son of God who said, "I am the way, and the truth, and the life" (John 14:6)—the Christ who summed up everything in one word, *LOVE:* "'You shall love the Lord your God with all your heart, and with all your soul, and with all your mind, and with all your strength.... You shall love your neighbor as yourself" (Mark 12:30-31). If we say we love others, then we must incarnate this love toward them. In doing that, we will prove God's continuous involvement in human history for, then, our hands will be God's, always ready to do God's work.

When God's eyes become our eyes, his ears our ears, his will our will, his hands our hands, it becomes up to us, in a sense, to co-create a world according to God's desire and will. Let us take a close look at our hands. What a responsibility is in our hands! "A new creation" is in the making.

"Surely the Lord is in this place—and [we] did not know it!" (Genesis 28:16). This place is also the "new creation" in the making. We are in it. We are it.

The essence of Jesus' philosophy is to see with God's eye. There is no greater philosophy for us, for others, and for humanity than to see reality with God's eye. That is the truth.

By Way of Conclusion

Truth exists whether we like it or not.

Do not believe those who tell you that truth does not exist. Why should you believe them if what they are saying is not true anyway, since they just said there was no truth? For a while, their "truth" may serve them well, socially, financially, and even "religiously." Counting on cunning compromises and on wearing appropriate masks is not the way to the fullness of life; truth is.

It is in the nature of truth not to move according to the world, but to move the world. A person of truth refuses to be edited by society. A person of truth leaves the greatest impact on his or her society.

Do we know who we truly are? Our very lives, more than our words, are the answer to this age-old question.

If we are created in the image of God, only in God do we discover the truth about ourselves. Christianity is not knowledge about God; it is knowledge in God. God is love. We are unable to know this truth except by, in, and with love. In *The Cloud of Unknowing*, an enduring classic of Christian spirituality that was written in the fourteenth century, we read: "By love God may be caught and held: by thinking never." This is how critical was the "[Having] the mind of Christ" (1 Corinthians 2:16) of Paul. God knows about ourselves more than we, ourselves, know about ourselves. God created us for love.

Truth is truth when it is according to God's plan and to the way the divine plan is unfolding. Our own individual destiny, as well as the whole destiny of humankind, is christological in essence. That's the truth. Aren't we in the image of God? Therefore, a transfiguration in Christ should be expected. God's grace is available. How we are going to respond to it remains to be seen. Maximus the Confessor (580–662) says: "See how the Lord has given us the power to become eternally the children of God; henceforth our salvation is in our will."

The age of the complexities of life in which we live needs to capture God's truth—the truth that transforms and heals souls, minds, hearts, and bodies. Since we cannot be "know-it-all" and have "black and white" knowledge of everything, we need a north star or a certain map to guide us in our struggles with reality. Dr. M. Scott Peck offers a helpful image:

> The less clearly we see the reality of the world—the more our minds are befuddled by falsehood, misperceptions, and illusions—the less able we will be to determine correct courses of action and make wise decisions. Our view of reality is like a map with which to negotiate the terrain of life. If the map is true and accurate, we will generally know where we are, and if we have decided where we want to go, we will generally know how to get there. If the map is false and inaccurate, we generally will be lost.

God's word is that north star and that map. Only God's word is true and absolute, yesterday, today, and forever (see Hebrews 13:8). Only this truth gives true freedom. The rest is truth telling, concept shifts, and human fluctuations. If it does not make reference to God, any system we create, with the hope that it will help in the betterment of the world, will sooner rather than later collapse under its deceptions and lies, bringing more miseries to humankind. This is also the truth. A system or a state may provide some dignity to a person. But only God makes every person a person of dignity.

Mystics and saints often used silence instead of speech to express truth. They knew that silence—the gaps in the midst of a speech—is essential for communication to work. Their lives were more eloquent than the limitations of language to bear witness to the truth. They lived truth. They lived it in words, and especially in between the words—in the eloquent silence that gives meaning to the words. To do so was not, is not, and will never be an easy task. Apart from a few exceptions, a person of truth often pays a high price for witnessing to the truth, because neither the right nor the left knows where to classify him or her. Truth is not subject to classifications and limitations.

Truth is a set journey toward the one who said, "I am the way, and the truth, and the life" (John 14:6). It is the way toward the Way that leads to true Life. It is the truth that transforms profoundly and radically, because it sets everything it touches on fire—the fire of the Holy Spirit.

Integrity calls people to know who they truly are, be at home with their true selves, and shape the world in their image, which is a reflection of the image of God. By closely following Christ, one does not go astray, as mystic and theologian Richard of St. Victor (d. 1173) suggested: "If you are in a hurry to reach higher things, you will go safely if truth goes ahead of you. Without truth your labour is in vain. Truth does not want to deceive, and so it cannot be deceived. If you do not want to go astray, follow Christ." When we follow Christ, we start to see as God sees. Here, Meister Eckhart (1260–1328), one of history's great mystics, cannot help but say unambiguously:

It is your destiny to see as God sees,
to know as God knows,
to feel as God
feels.
How is this possible? How?
Because divine love cannot defy its very self…
Every object, every creature, every man, woman and child
has a soul and it is the destiny of all,
to see as God sees, to know as God knows,
to feel as God feels, to Be
as God
is.

So, a repeated lie does not make it truth. It is truth that makes a lie a "true" lie. That is the truth.

Not telling the truth is only one way of lying. The other, more horrible and detrimental way is lying with our very lives. Indeed, the immense and unforgivable catastrophe in one's life is to conclude at one's deathbed that "my life was a lie." This, indeed, will be a catastrophe for that individual and for society. "Devotion to Truth is," as Gandhi put it, "the sole justification for our existence."

Epilogue

"Everything Begins in Mysticism and Ends in Politics"

Charles Péguy (1873–1914) was a French poet and writer. He wrote a provocative line to identify the foundational starting point that pulls together faith and politics. He wrote: "Everything begins in mysticism and ends in politics," when we usually think that the reverse would be the correct way, to begin with politics then to try to figure out how religion can fit in. The truth is that a real and transformative change in politics is a spiritual journey that starts in the inward hearts. Then the outward social and economic structures, the constitutions, laws, and the different rules that run our lives will be transformed accordingly. Faith has real and tangible consequences in the world, and that includes politics.

Therefore, if we start our life journey from an inward mystical point and we let God's love flow through us, everything else will change accordingly, and our politics would be the correct politics. But if we start with politics, chances are that all we do will reflect our self-interests, ambitions, and inflated egos. This, then, would be the worst kind of politics there is. We are supposed to start not with what we are doing but with who and what we really are, our true selves. We are children of God first, and everything we do should be the fruit of that reality. Well-written constitutions will not make us "light of the world," and good laws will not make us "salt of the earth." Having the "mind of Christ" does.

The mystical eye is different from the ordinary eye. While the ordinary eye is content with what it sees at the surface, the mystical eye sees underneath the surface; it sees the realities of the mind, heart, soul, and the divine. This is what matters most. It is, as Teilhard de Chardin put it, the "true mystical science, that really matters…obviously, many primitive intuitions have been corrupted and blunted by civilizations and speculation… however, mysticism remains the great science and the great art, the only power capable of synthesizing the riches accumulated by other forms of human activities." Concepts may obscure the vision by their heaviness and complexity to the point that they may even blind the eye. The mystical eye is unobstructed, unclogged, and unobligated.

To see with a mystical eye and to be a revolutionary are not opposite at all. In fact, they can be best allies. No wonder why most mystics in human history were not only tolerated or simply rejected by society, they were also condemned, persecuted, and sometimes executed, and that is because they can never be supporters of the establishment and the status quo.

A real mysticism and a real revolution deal with a radical change. Both of them face the human condition as it is, and both of them want to grasp the secret of a sick society. Both of them are concerned with freeing their fellow human beings from their alienations, fears, and paralysis. Both of them call to arms to fight the petty fantasies of the egos and, by their far-reaching vision, create an atmosphere of harmony and reconciliation. Both of them, by digging deep into the very core of things and touching the human hearts, aim to change things around. Both of them know well that no radical change in society will be possible unless there is a change of heart first.

To see means to discern, understand, and develop a worldview from a different angle; it is not the natural seeing of the common physical eye, but a seeing of an altogether different order.

To see means to reconstruct the world and co-create reality according to one's own mystical perception, in the image and likeness of one's already transformed heart. Reality will be as perfect and peaceful as the quality of our seeing is. "Our future is in our own hands," Teilhard affirms. Therefore, as he also says, "A new way of seeing, combined with a new way of acting – that is what we need." Consequently, all these categories – conservative, liberal, right, left, fascist, communist… which label and rule our lives, should be put to rest in the history books, and new patterns of human relationships should be created in the direction of the human and the forward.

To see does not only mean to survive, but to ascend into a higher state of existence in unity with an immense variety of interdependent cultures, activities, and civilizations. Peace, then, may move forward by using essentially the human beings' psychic powers, which can be maximized by contemplation. Contemplation has the potential to increase the psychic temperature of the noosphere (the thinking envelope of the earth) by nurturing the most profoundly human and by quickening an increased consciousness.

To see means to change the way we think, the way we imagine, the way we perceive things. It means that we have to change our angle and mode of vision, our attitude, and our approach to life. It means that we have to change.

To see deep, clear, big, forward, upward, and far, very far, is the way not only to survive, but also to real peace. "To see or to perish," Teilhard de Chardin reminds us.

When we open our eyes and see with our physical eyes, we usually see appearances. When we close our physical eyes and see with our mind, heart, and soul, we usually see what lies under the appearances. We see the connection, the whole, the universal, and what matters most, the essence of reality.

We see what we want to see, after all; the world is not better or worse than we want it to be. We may see the same things over and over again, but each time we may see them differently. The truth is that we seldom see things as they are; we see them as we are. That is why, when we change our mind, our priorities, our values, and our references, we see different realities altogether.

What does this mean, existentially?

It means that we are not just observers of a so-called reality, or its photographers, or its recorders. We are active participants, artists, co-creators, or destroyers. When we watch the evening news, what do we really watch? We do not really watch the facts of the event; we watch rather how the reporter conveyed the facts. It is really an interpretation, if not a translation, of the facts.

We can be co-creators as well. For the sake of more clarity, let us try this little exercise: "see" God, really and existentially, everywhere: in the sun, the stars, the flowers, the doves, the fire, the water, the desert, the woods, the mustard seed, the faces of every man and woman, and in your own circumstances. Do you still see all these the same way? When you realize that God is the loving force of the whole, you immediately see how interrelated, interconnected, and interdependent we all are. At this very moment, the walls of polarization, limits, frontiers, restrictions, prejudices, and narrow-mindedness collapse. Whether we know it or not, the way we live our life has been influenced, controlled, and conditioned by our personal philosophy, our dominant way of thinking. If the world is a reflection of what we see, what we see makes our world as well; what we see is how we see it. It has been said that "The way you look at things is the most powerful force in shaping your life. In a vital sense, perception is reality," wrote John O'Donohue, and he also wrote, "It is a startling truth that how you see and what you see determine how and who you will be." Didn't Michelangelo see the statue of David in the marble first?

This is the way it is. Every time we close our eyes to see the reality with our mind, heart, and soul, we open our eyes to see things transformed. Our outlook on life has changed in such a way that now we see a world without limited horizons. Our vision is now universal, and the scope of our consciousness has become open to the infinite.

The consequences of this operation are enormous. As soon as we begin to recognise the essential under the appearances and what is important over what is secondary, we will start to see our consciousness extended into the universal realities, the common good, the human rights, and the deep connection between everyone and everything.

To see that unity is a complete interdependence of the immense varieties of cultures, civilizations, societies, histories, and ethnicities; that, because we organically "interbe," we will survive together or we will die together; that even though they lost their humanness in war, human beings ironically gained more ground in regard to unification, and they also learned what is essential and what is not.

To see that, when we want to see the truth, we need educated and trained, healthy eyes. Otherwise we will live in darkness. The Gospel says: "The eye is the lamp of the body. So, if your eye is healthy, your whole body will be full of light; but if your eye is unhealthy, your whole body will be full of darkness. If then the light in you is darkness, how great is the darkness!"

To see that, while retaining confidence in reason, logic, and syllogism, we know how to transcend the ordinary way of thinking and think vertically by going down, down, down. The further we can go in our consciousness to the centre of our soul. There we can find our true selves and others in God. There we can find all in God and God in all. Peace might be right there. It is there.

If for Hamlet, "To be or not to be" was the question, "To see or not to see" would be the other big question whose answer affects our entire life. "Where there is no vision, the people perish," the Book of the Proverbs (29:18, KJV) warns us. "To see or to perish," Teilhard would echo the Bible.

To see that, when one sees far enough, one sees unity and, further, one sees God.

However, and in order to get there, we should have the "mind of Christ" (I Corinthians 2:16).

About the Author

Dr. Jean Maalouf's books (more than 50 books and essays) have been published in the United States of America, Canada, Mexico, Colombia, France, Spain, Portugal, the Philippines, and India. Also, he has written many articles on topics of religion, spirituality, mysticism (Eastern and Western), philosophy, psychology, and peace and social issues for journals and magazines such as *Catholic Digest, Celebration, National Herald* (New Delhi), *Peace Research Reviews* (Canada), *Praying, Revue des Sciences Philosophiques et Théologiques* (Paris), *Spirit & Life, Spiritual Life,* and *Teilhard Perspective.* He is a member of several professional associations that include the American Academy of Religion, American Teilhard Association, Association des Amis de P. Teilhard de Chardin (Paris), The Authors Guild, Contemplative Outreach, Centering Prayer, National Writers Union, Fellowship of Catholic Scholars, Catholic Writers Guild, and The Society of Christian Philosophers.

The messages in Dr. Maalouf's writings seem deeply personal, as if they were written just for the person who is reading them, and yet they are timeless and universal. His works were hailed by critics with terms such as these: "Jean Maalouf brings his experience as doctor of philosophy and humanities to bear in works of spirituality. His focus is one of gentle revolution in human development," "Maalouf has written in the style of Meister Eckhart, John of the Cross, and St. Irenaeus," and "Maalouf's gift for writing about the most sublime truths in the most simple language allows him... to touch and transform the hearts of believers and non-believers alike." He is blessed with the art of provoking thoughts that inspire new choices, influence decisions, and get the attention of both the religious and secular worlds, as well as the academic and the non-academic ones. In a culture that often relegates God to loftiness, he knows how to provide compelling images of God in unexpected places, in the most ordinary aspects of our daily lives. It is no wonder then that he sees, because of the continuous Incarnation in everyday life, how one can transform his or her daily life through moments of grace.

➢ Publications by Dr. Jean Maalouf

Publications in English

Awakening to the Philosophy of Jesus
Bold Prayers from the Heart
The Burning Flame of Love
Change Your World: Awakening to the Power of Truth – Beauty – Simplicity - Change
Christmas Shock: The Human Experience of God
The Divine Milieu: A Spiritual Classic for Today and Tomorrow (Essay)
The Essential Connection: Living Prayer
Experiencing Jesus with Mother Teresa

Fully Alive: God's Prescription for a Happier and Healthier Life

Heal Your Life: awakening to the Power of Faith – Hope – Love - Prayer

The Healing Power of Beauty

The Healing Power of Change

The Healing Power of Faith

The Healing Power of Forgiveness

The Healing Power of Friendship

The Healing Power of Gratitude

The Healing Power of Hope

The Healing Power of Joy

The Healing Power of Kindness

The Healing Power of Love

The Healing Power of Peace

The Healing Power of Prayer

The Healing Power of Purpose

The Healing Power of Simplicity

The Healing Power of Truth

I Can Tell God Anything: Living Prayer

If We Just See What They See: Peace According to Albert Einstein, Thomas Merton, Pope John XXIII, Thick Nhat Hanh, Mahatma Gandhi, Teilhard de Chardin, Mother Teresa of Calcutta

Intimacies: The Miracle of Love

I've Got One Life to Live: Radiant Health God's Way

Jesus Laughed and Other Reflections on Being Human

The Little Way: Fresh Air for the Soul — A Retreat with Saint Thérèse of Lisieux

Live a Life That Matters: Awakening to the Power of Purpose — Kindness — Forgiveness — Friendship

Making All Things New

Mother Teresa: Essential Writings (Editor)

The New Tower of Babel

Pathways: Finding God in the Present Moment

Pope John XXIII: Essential Writings (Editor)

Practicing the Presence of the Living God: A Retreat with Brother Lawrence of the Resurrection

Praying with Mother Teresa

Teilhard and the Feminine (Essay)

Teilhard de Chardin: Reconciliation in Christ (Editor)

Teilhard's Proposition for Peace: Rediscovering the Fire

Touch a Single Leaf: Teilhard and Peace

Touchstones for Peace (Essay)

Transformation in Prayer: 99 Sayings by M. Basil Pennington (Editor)

Where Has God Gone?

Your New Adventure: Make the Most of the Rest of Your Life

Contributor to:

Encyclopedia of Catholic Social Thought, Social Science, and Social Policy

Publications in French

Le Mystère du Mal dans L'Oeuvre de Teilhard de Chardin

Teilhard de Chardin et le mystère du mal. Evolutionisme? Stoïcisme? Christocentrisme? (Essay)

Le Réenchantement du Monde (Co-author)

La Terre Est Mon Pays (Co-author)

Publications in Spanish (Translated from English)
Dile a Dios Lo Que Sientes: Oración Desde La Vida
El Poder Sanador De La Alegría
El Poder Sanador De La Amistad
El Poder Sanador De La Bondad
El Poder Sanador De La Esperanza
El Poder Sanador De La Fe
El Poder Sanador De La Oración
El Poder Sanador Del Amor
El Poder Sanador De La Paz
El Poder Sanador Del Perdón
El Poder Sanador De Tener Un Propósito
Juan XXIII: Escritos Esenciales
Madre Teresa de Calcuta: Escritos Esenciales
Orando Con La Madre Teresa
Orando Con La Madre Teresa De Calcuta

Publications in Portuguese (Translated from English)
O Poder Da Cura Pela Alegria
O Poder Da Cura Pela Amizade
O Poder Da Cura Pela Amor
O Poder Da Cura Pela Paz